INK FAMILY TREE

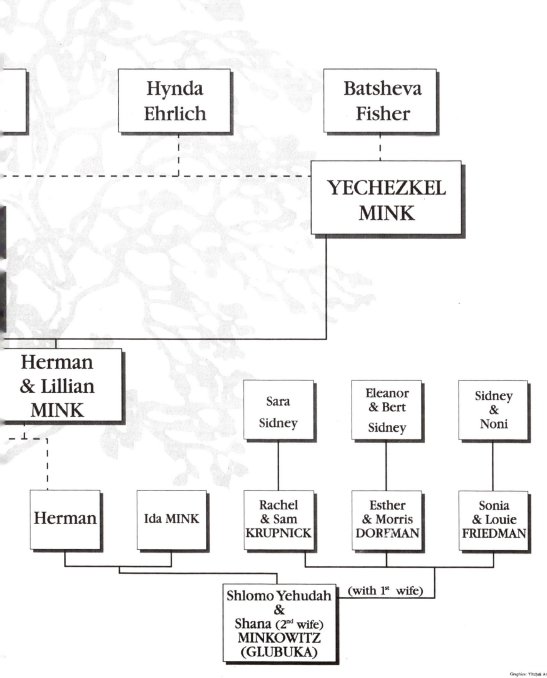

Hynda Ehrlich

Batsheva Fisher

YECHEZKEL MINK

Herman & Lillian MINK

Sara Sidney

Eleanor & Bert Sidney

Sidney & Noni

Herman

Ida MINK

Rachel & Sam KRUPNICK

Esther & Morris DORFMAN

Sonia & Louie FRIEDMAN

(with 1st wife)

Shlomo Yehudah & Shana (2nd wife) MINKOWITZ (GLUBUKA)

Graphics: Yitzhak Atlas (TA)

HOW A JEWISH SCRAPMAN RECYCLED HIS LIFE

YECHEZKEL MINK

HOW A JEWISH SCRAPMAN RECYCLED HIS LIFE

YECHEZKEL MINK

gefen גפן
publishing house בית הוצאה לאור

JERUSALEM ♦ NEW YORK

Typesetting: Marzel A.S., Jerusalem

Cover Concept: Yechezkel Mink

Cover Design: Gil Friedman / Gefen

Front cover photo: Bacharach Portrait Studios, New York

Back cover photo: Dr. Richard Jaffe, Old City, Jerusalem

ISBN 965 229 184 6

Gefen Publishing House Ltd.   Gefen Books
POB 36004, Jerusalem   12 New St., Hewlett,
91360 Israel   NY 11557, U.S.A.
972-2-5380247   516-295-2805
E-mail: isragefen@netmedia.net.il

Printed in Israel
Send for our free catalogue

Dedicated to
my zadah (grandfather) z"l
Nahum Haim Gering of Bialystok, Poland.

Grandfather

Acknowledgements

To my cousins Lisa and Richie Aroll (Jerusalem)
who assisted me in assembling this book.

Libby Werthan (Jerusalem),
for encouraging me to start the project.

Contents

DIVINE
INTERVENTION

For the past four years I have enormously enjoyed and profited sitting in on the classes of Rabbi-Professor David Gottlieb at Yeshiva Ohr Sameach here in Jerusalem. His almost limitless knowledge encompassing Chumash, Talmud, Jewish practices, and holiday and daily rituals, plus his versatility in secular subjects ranging from philosophy (his doctoral thesis) to science, advanced math, literature and endless dissertations on remote studies are truly spectacular to his student of 70 summers. One phrase he often uses to explain the unexplainable is Divine Intervention, which I will henceforth refer to as D.I. It recently occurred to me, Yechezkel-Charles Jerry Mink, a Bal Teshuva, former Long Island, NY scrap metal dealer, often married and proud father of three accomplished children as well as grandchildren, that I may also have experienced D.I.

Please share this story and judge for yourself...

PREFACE

Writing my life story, I came to realize that the formula would be a series of events. It came to me – they all fitted together, as though each was part of an abstract pattern. I choose to think it was a force sent by my zadah, Reb Nahum Haim Gering of Bialystok, Poland.

PROGRAM

List of Personalities in This Amazing, Interesting Scenario in a Chronological Order of Sorts.

    Supplied at *No Extra Charge*

    Enabling You to Follow This Action-Packed Drama.

Leading Personalities in Saga

Yechezkel – Surname unknown; author named in memory of great-grandfather at brit.

Nahum Haim Gering – Maternal grandfather; home: Bialystok, Poland. Major presence in saga.

Shoshana Gering – Daughter of original Yechezkel; grandmother to author.

Shlomo Yehuda Minkowitz – Paternal grandfather; home: Glubuka, Lithuania. A leading citizen??

Shana Minkowitz – Grandmother; thought to be Shlomo's 2nd wife and very petite.

Lillian Chaya Leah Mink – Revered mother of author.

Herman Eliezer Chaim Mink – Father of author.

Yechezkel Charles Jerry Mink – Author; _____.

                                    (reader may fill in description)

Mohel at Unity Hospital, Brooklyn, NY – Name withheld on purpose. He did a haphazard job.

Selma a.k.a. Sue Lubkin – Sister and long-suffering; trying to explain author to her public.

Arthur Lubkin – Attorney; husband to sister Sue.

Dr. Lisa Ellen Mink Shulman – 1st-born daughter via Gloria.

Dr. Mitchell Neal Mink – 1st-born son via Gloria.

Jacqueline Leah Mink, M.A. – 2nd-born daughter via Bayla.

Gloria Stamberg Mink – Wife #1.

Bayla (Bea) Siflinger Mink – Wife #2.

Aviva Ranani (Mink surname removed in divorce agreement) – Wife #3.

Hynda Ehrlich Mink – Wife #4.

BatSheva Fisher Mink – Wife #5.

HOW I DECIDED TO WRITE
THIS AUTOBIOGRAPHY

1985. I was employed by Bank Leumi in a unique position. The bank had opened a number of 1 or 2-man offices in the major hotels in Israel. (My position was in the Plaza, Jerusalem; to be covered in another chapter.)

One morning a Dr. David Schnall entered our office. Are you Mr. Mink? I'm here on assignment for the newspaper, Newsday, on Long Island, to author an article about former Long Islanders who have made aliyah. Can you give me an hour of your time? Why not?!? There was to be a second interviewee, Rabbi Jeremy Fenster. Dr. Schnall, an Orthodox Jew, wore several hats besides his kippa. He was an associate professor at C.W. Post College and Long Island University, both on Long Island, NY and an activist in Jewish affairs. He had been referred by Rabbi Meyer Fendel (see chapter: Buying the Torah). They davened at the same shul in West Hempstead, LI, NY, that of Rabbi Sholom Gold. That afternoon, he joined me at home for the interview. After hearing my saga, plus taking several pictures, he remarked, "I have enough here for five articles," and departed. I heard nothing for at least six months. I assumed it was another non-starter.

One morning, my sister Selma called with alarm. "Jerry, you're famous!" My story appeared as a full page spread plus a 10-12 inch picture in the magazine section of the paper Newsday. Within a short time, I began receiving letters and calls from people I hadn't touched base with in 30-40 years. Several calls and letters also came from single women. (He stated I was divorced and comfortable. I hate that expression.)

Yechezkel Mink, on terrace of his apartment overlooking the Western Wall, says that living so near the sacred wall is "overwhelming."

New Life In Jerusalem's Old City

By David J. Schnall

"I DON'T care what Barnum said. For a Jew, this is the greatest show on earth." The speaker is Yeheskel Mink, a tall, dark-haired, middle-aged man in a white shirt and tan slacks. He gestures toward the plaza below and the massive wall that stands at its far end. "I feel as if I'm living partly in the 20th Century and partly in the time of King David," he says with a smile.

And, indeed, the Rova, the popular term for the restored Jewish Quarter of Jerusalem's Old City, is a place of stark contrasts, where the old and new collide. Perhaps nothing more clearly underlines the point than Mink's presence. Like many other Americans who have settled there among the native Israelis, he is helping to infuse the Rova with new life and a vastly different world perspective.

While its population is being reshaped by American immigrants such as Mink, the Rova itself has been undergoing dramatic alterations. Sleek apartment buildings have risen alongside stone walls that once marked Jerusalem's boundaries in the Eighth Century BC; synagogues have been restored; a main thoroughfare is being revitalized.

From the balcony of the apartment where he lives alone — an apartment whose terrace overlooks the Western Wall — Mink can see some of the changes occurring. If he looks hard enough, he can also see the small scraps of paper that believers have inserted in the cracks between the mammoth lower stones of the wall. On each note is inscribed the special needs of some visitor. It is the Lord's private mail slot, as it were.

"To *daven* here, to pray here during the holidays . . . ," Mink says. "Some people do it only once in a lifetime. I do it all the time." His face softens and his eyes fairly sparkle as he recalls the experience. Then he laughs with embarrassment and says, "Living in the shadow of the Kotel, the Western Wall, is overwhelming and overpowering. I'm afraid to walk around the house naked. Really, I can feel the presence."

All that remains of the ancient Second Temple of Israel stands in the Jewish Quarter, but it's little more than a retaining wall built by Herod, the notorious pretender. Still, it was to this Temple Mount that early Israelites made pilgrimages three times a year. Today, their descendants come here from all parts of the world seeking blessings, inspiration and unity with the ancients. Asked if he ever feels blase about living so close to the wall, he says, "It blows my mind every time I go down there. Almost every day, something happens to me here and, like, my batteries are recharged."

David J. Schnall of West Hempstead is an associate professor at LIU, C.W. Post Campus, and author of "Beyond the Green Line: Israeli Settlements West of the Jordan."

On my next visit to the States, I contacted Dr. Schnall – who had left his card – to thank him for the article and invited him for a kosher lunch. At the meeting, Schnall came up with a proposal. He would like to write my biography. He thought my life was quite unique. This was all very flattering. I answered, "Go ahead." Schnall said he would get back to me. He did.

The Terms:

1. I would underwrite a one-month visit for him and his family to Israel, cost about $5,000.
2. He had spoken to a publisher. (I discovered later it's referred to as Vanity Press.) They were willing to publish the biography.
3. I would have to guarantee the book would sell a minimum of 1,500 copies, at $12 per book; a total of $18,000.

J. Mink, "What if they don't sell?"

Dr. Schnall, "Well, Mr. Mink, you can distribute them or sell them yourself."

Bottom line: an investment with a downside risk of $23,000.

It sounded pretentious. I felt obligated to ask my three children how they felt; it dealt with their lives as well. Surprisingly, they said "Go for it."

I finally came to the conclusion it was not in keeping with my general outlook and I had better things to do with $23,000. And who knows if I would like Dr. Schnall's finished product.

So, I decided to do it myself – Mink the Autobiographer.

WHY I DECIDED
TO WRITE THIS BOOK

The answer is mostly in the chapters, The Apartment. During the seventeen years I have dwelt in this location, directly opposite the Wall, literally hundreds of visitors have inquired as to how I stumbled onto this home. As I described in that chapter, I repeated the missa[1] an infinite number of times. This led to an internal evaluation that it wasn't an accident but predestined, or Divine Intervention.

I have always enjoyed correspondence, even sending my opinions via Letters to the Editor. Eight years ago I wrote the pamphlet 40 Years They Wandered (noted in a later chapter), and when my friend Guy Bernfeld began publishing his monthly "In Jerusalem," I wrote several articles for him. I conceived the idea of "Only in Israel" and submitted two small items, now reproduced in this book. Plus, at each effort I had the more than capable assistance of my cousins, the Arolls, of Har Nof, Jerusalem, who made aliyah in 1987. In effect, the team was in place.

After I completed the apartment chapter – see the Jerusalem Post ad – (which I honestly was pleased with), I began showing it to friends, even sending copies to my children in the USA. One of the people, Libby Werthan of Baka, Jerusalem, formerly of Nashville, Tennessee, exclaimed after reading the chapter: "I liked your style. I want to read more. Sit down and continue. Don't be afraid; just let it pour out."

---

1. missa, missas – story, stories.

I did sit down that day and began listing other chapters in my life. I thought it interesting that they were a synopsis of tales that I have been repeating for the past 50 years. As my old dear friend Larry Roth (to be mentioned often, says): "You're a great storyteller!" This ongoing labor of love has lasted two years and pressed forward with the coming of my seventieth birthday in August 1997. I hope you enjoy my missas!

DATE OF BIRTH

Born in Brooklyn, NY, on August 14, 1927, I feel mine was an oft repeated saga. My mother came from a very Orthodox home in Bialystok, Poland. My father was at best not involved religiously, and their arranged marriage in the States was senseless, for lack of a fiercer word. But mother gave me direction till she left this world when I was 19.

A prevailing story in our home, one with endless chapters, was the saga of my Zadah (grandfather), Nahum Haim Gering, said to have been a tzaddik in his time. One of the episodes, as related, follows.

A number of his siblings emigrated to the States but Reb Nahum Haim would not go to the treifa medina[1] – the USA.

Where did they get the money for the journey, including my mother's? It seems his sister, Bessy (probably Batia) Alexander was married to a prosperous businessman – thanks to the Prohibition period (no comment) – but, unfortunately, childless. Any D.I. here? So over a period of 15 or 20 years she sent funds overseas to bring the family to America.

When it came to Reb Nahum Haim's turn, he made a decision to make aliyah to Palestine. The timing could not have been worse. It was 1929 and the infamous Hebron massacre of Jews by Arab mobs had occurred.

When my savta, Shoshana, read about this, she exclaimed, "Are you taking us to Palestine to be killed by the Arabs?" at which point Nahum Haim's dream

---

1. treifa medina – unkosher country.

vanished. They remained in Poland and the money was given for tzedaka.[1] Both passed on prior to the Shoah, and Hitler murdered my Aunts Rifka and Faigel, my mother's two younger siblings, and their respective families.

---

1. tzedaka – charity.

THE GIFT

At the age of 4 or 5 I was the recipient of a gift from Nahum Haim, a set of tefillin and a siddur with the inscription in Yiddish: To my grandson, Yechezkel, from his Zadah Nahum Haim in Bialystok. I used the tefillin daily from my bar mitzah till I entered the US Navy. On my discharge two things changed: I had discontinued the practice of davening every morning and my mother passed on. Somewhere in the back of my conscience was the awareness that I was an heir apparent to my Zadah's wishes and responsible for some continuity of his faith and religious observance.

THE APARTMENT –
THE MABBUL (DOWNPOUR)

By the time of my aliyah, I was divorced from my second wife Bayla, and remarried for a short six months to Aviva, a sabra Tel Aviv attorney. The less said the better. Soon after I moved to Yamit in the Sinai (after a horrendous business experience with significant financial losses). With the return of the Sinai to Egypt, I was dispossessed from Yamit and moved up to Jerusalem.

D.I. again??? Waiting one evening in the Plaza Hotel in Jerusalem for an appointment, I struck up a conversation with Rabbi Mordechai Goldstein of the Diaspora Yeshiva, and soon after began to study. I spent the following two years in the yeshiva and basically converted my life-style to an Orthodox stream.

On an annual trip to the States to visit with family and friends, I met Hynda. She was in her late 30's, teaching in the NYC school system, caught up in the NYC pseudo excitement, going nowhere and concerned about the ticking of the biological clock to start a family.

The following summer she came to Israel and got caught up in the romance and excitement of the Israel scene, and we were soon married. We rented an apartment in Beit Hakerem, Jerusalem, but she decided we should buy an apartment immediately and settle in to raise a family. Unfortunately, Hynda had physical problems and the reproductive process never occurred. In order to keep her occupied, we took over a small hat and shmatta business; importing and selling kept her busy going back and forth to the States.

Still, her demand to buy our own place persisted and was paramount in her mind. Finally, an agent found her an apartment on Rechov Caspi in northern Talpiot, an area of Jerusalem. Against my better judgment she demanded we buy the place. I retained attorney Donald Zisquit and inquired why the building was unoccupied, without electricity or water. The agent had an explanation for everything but Zisquit insisted we retain an architect. We soon discovered that the builder had overbuilt, totally enclosing patios, and converted the miklat (shelter) into a 3-room additional apartment, which meant the City authorities would not give them a C of O (approval to occupy). Being hounded continually and trying to maintain "sholem bayit" (peace at home), I agreed to buy this lemon, despite my strong reservations.

On contacting the seller's attorney, I discovered the owner was returning to Germany that same day, where he resided. Dreading the possibility of not completing this purchase, I ran to attorney Zisquit's office. He drew up a Zichron Devarim (letter of intent) and I withdrew a $10,000 bank check from my account and ran like a madman to catch the Lufthansa flight at Ben Gurion Airport. On the way the skies literally opened up; the rain was so intense the windshield wipers were inoperative, and I was forced to stop beneath an overpass and wait for 15 minutes for the ferocity of the storm to pass. Again, I resumed the chase, arrived at the airport sopping wet, with the check and contract in my hand. Naturally, the owner was surprised to see me. I requested he sign the document and take the deposit check. When he saw the check was in dollars, he said "What am I to do with a dollar check? Send me that amount in DM."

So there I stood, soaking wet, on the check-in line at Lufthansa and again no deal. Needless to say, when I returned home that evening Hynda was irate and inconsolable: "This proves you really don't want to buy us a home." Later, lying in bed, the reality of what was happening struck me. After a sleepless night I told her, "I don't want that apartment at any price, it's madness...."

Could this have been D.I.????

THE APARTMENT –
THE JERUSALEM POST AD

A few weeks later, Hynda again left on a buying trip to the States. Being home alone, I read the Friday paper thoroughly and was taken by a three-line ad in the Real Estate Section: "Desperate; We must sell our beautiful home overlooking the Western Wall. Call _____."

Sunday morning I called and naturally asked the price. When the lady said $275,000 I answered it was outside of our budget and was about to hang up. She literally screamed, "Please don't hang up. We are really desperate to sell. First come and see our home." Another case of D.I., I'm certain. At that time I was employed by Bank Leumi, which meant I had the afternoon off. I drove over and when I walked out on the mirpesset (terrace) and saw the unbelievable sight of the entire Western Wall plus the 1st and 2nd Temple site, I became aware of D.I. without really understanding it. I gave them a small deposit after getting a 15% reduction. (I explained I first needed my wife's approval.) On her return, we met at the office of the vendor's attorney, and Hynda immediately began to haggle with the owners about leaving the phone-line (16 years ago it was a major hassle to get a new phone-line). She got up to leave the meeting. After excusing myself, I joined her outside and said, "Hynda, this is the apartment I was meant to buy with your approval or otherwise."

We bought it (without the phone) and two years later we divorced, allowing Hynda to return to her exciting life in the Big Apple. For the past 16 years I have had the good fortune of davening every morning with my Zadah's tefillin, looking over at the Har Habayit. The zechus[1] for this, I'm certain, is his...

Is there D.I.? You tell me.

---

1. zechus – merit.

THE APARTMENT – THE VISIT

During my adolescent and young adult years, I had always felt "more Jewish" than my peer group. When the War of Independence broke out in Israel in 1948, I was 21 and ideally suited to participate, but it did not happen.

Visiting the Wall, 1968, my eventual home

For years after I rationalized the many reasons I did not get involved. When the Six Day War began, I told my ex-wife Bayla "I have to go." But, to use her expression, "will you be taking along your golf clubs, tennis racket and bowling ball?" Again, non-participation; remember, it was all over in six days! A year later, July 1968, Yechezkel (Jerry) Mink decided it was time at least to visit Israel. So, with my Zadah's tefillin and siddur I eventually arrived on the obligatory visit to the "Wall." I put on my tefillin, said some brachot from *his* siddur[1] and turned around to take a picture of the churban (total destruction) at my back. (See picture.) That frame is the location where I've resided for the past 16 years. Any D.I.?

Five years later, during the Yom Kippur War, I finally did come over as a volunteer, and basically made decisions based on my experiences then to make aliyah. This I did 2½ years later.

It might be noted, when I came during the war, I made sure to have my Zadah's tefillin and siddur with me...

---

1. siddur – prayer book.

HOW CHARLES BECAME JERRY, THANKS TO UNCLE DOVID

I related elsewhere how my mother came to the U.S. thanks to the largesse of her Aunt Bessy Alexander.

On arrival, she was presented to the Patriarch of the family in the U.S., Uncle Dovid, the oldest brother of my Zadah's family, the Gerings, in Poland.

Shoshana and Nahum Haim Gering (my maternal grandparents), Bialystok

Dovid had arrived in the States a number of years earlier with his wife, Chaika (I think) and four children. They settled in Williamsburg, Brooklyn, in spite of my Zadah Nahum Haim's admonition about the treifa medina. Dovid and his family remained devoutly observant. Dovid always went about with a tall black kippa and Chaika was the only woman with a sheitel (wig) that I knew as a kid.

But Dovid's real forte was to have the family adopt names which he felt were appropriate. My mother and her sister had arrived in the States as Lillian and Dorothy Gering. Uncle Dovid deemed Gering was not Jewish-sounding enough, so he and his children became (the more Jewish) Blumbergs. My mother's branch of the family also became Blumberg. When my Uncle George arrived, he rejected Blumberg; his family remained Gering. Uncle George was made of tougher fabric.

When my mother brought me around to pay the duty visit to the Patriarch, her uncle, he inquired as to my name. Mama said Yechezkel – after her deceased grandfather on her mother Shoshana's side. Dovid approved of that. He asked, "Vos ruft em in English?" (What do you call him in English?) Mama replied, "Charles." Uncle Dovid immediately "poskind" (ruled) it not good. It was not a Jewish-sounding name, so he pinned the more Jewish-sounding name, Jerry, on me then and there. And it stuck. In fact, when Mama registered me in public school and took out my birth certificate, she realized that the name was Charles, which had been totally forgotten.

The oldest daughter of Dovid, Annie, married an observant man, Mordechai Aroll. Strangely enough, the three younger children, Jack, Alex and Ruth, lived at home and never married. Jack was a man-about-town, and not that religious. Alex seemed to be rather abstract or playing with a short deck. And poor Ruth was diagnosed in her 20's as a victim of brain cancer and was scarred for life by this event, despite having a successful operation.

Which brings me around to the Aroll family. Annie had two sons, Harold and Herbert. Harold was an accountant, not very observant, and passed on at a young age. Herbert was a brilliant student, graduated law school, and passed the Bar at the age of 20. Being very observant, he refused to work on Shabbos (the Sabbath), as was normal in the 1930's. Thus, he never pursued a legal career. After serving in the army in World War II, he took a position with the NYC Social Services Dept, which did not entail Shabbos work. He eventually rose to a very senior position in city government, and remained religious. He married an observant woman, Sylvia, and they had two sons, Morton and Richard. Both are also observant. Richie, his lovely wife and six children made aliyah (moved to Israel) and reside in Har Nof, Jerusalem. Richie is a Breslov Hassid and his older sons are right-wing religious – black fedoras and all. So my Great-Uncle Dovid did make his mark, besides name changing, as a courier of the religious Torah life from Bialystok, Poland to the USA, and now Eretz Israel.

Perhaps Great-Uncle Dovid was right. I should have stuck with just Yechezkel – that's what I'm called today.

Jerry Mink, age 3,
growing up in New York

WHAT WAS THE DEPRESSION LIKE?
AND ITS EFFECTS ON MY FAMILY

What I can recall are apartments renting for $20 and $35 a month.
Salaries starting at $6, $8, and $10 and $20 a week.
$0.02 and $0.03 newspapers; Sunday paper – $0.05.
Subway Rides – $0.05. A malted milk – $0.05.
Coca Cola – $0.03 at a fountain

Money was tight and precious. When I was five, Mama arranged for me to have private Hebrew school lessons in a rabbi's home twice a week. The bill? $0.75 a month.

I'd like to record the story of my cousin Sidney Friedman, Papa's nephew and his elder sister Sonia's son.

Sidney F. was a friend of my cousin Herbert Aroll, spoken of in the chapter How Charles Became Jerry. They attended Talmud Torah[1] together. Brilliant as Herb Aroll was, graduating law school and passing the New York State bar exam at age 20, my cousin Sidney F. was phenomenal. He graduated high school at 14 and won a scholarship. He attended Columbia University, an Ivy League School. (His parents were really poor; his father Louie Friedman was an occasional house painter.) Sid graduated at age 18, with a Master's Degree in psychology.

The next step for Sid was obviously medical school (his dream). But in reality impossible.

---

1. Talmud Torah – after school religious instruction.

1. There were clear-cut restrictions on Jewish admissions in the 1930's and in addition the Friedmans lacked contacts to facilitate entry into med school, usually assisted via alumni.
2. Besides, his parents could never afford the tuition. There was family talk of finding a rich girl shidduch so Sid could attend a medical university in Europe. But nothing came of it.

What a waste of brains. I recall the American black population in the 70's and 80's proclaiming: "To waste a mind is a crime." Let's consider for a moment the thousands of Sidney Friedmans that never reached their potential during the Depression years. And lest we forget the one million Jewish children turned into ashes by the *cultured* Germans in WWII. How many Chagalls, Isaac Sterns, Jonas Salks, and perhaps Einsteins who also never reached their potential.

In despair, and to assist his parents, Sid went to work for a neighbor, a Mr. Bakst as I remember, on a truck route delivering pickles and condiments. In time, Sid learned that the Federal Government was hiring college graduates to work in Washington, D.C. He applied and was eventually assigned to the Navy department at $1,200 a year. He met a nice Jewish girl, Nonie, also employed at a government office in Washington. They were married. World War II came along. Sid was called into service. After several years he returned to his Federal Government job. When he reached retirement in the 1970's, Sid had risen to the highest civil service rank as senior job analyst for the Navy department. He now lives comfortably in San Diego, CA. He and Nonie have two children. The old-timers say *those were the good old days* when a $ was a $. Don't believe them. Life was worse than difficult.

Postscript

The menu of prices is still astonishing:

A postcard stamp – $0.01. First class mail – $0.03;

Local movie admission – $0.10.

To stimulate use of electricity, the Consolidated Edison Company in New York City sold small home appliances, toasters, electric irons, etc. I remember Mama purchasing them one at a time and going weekly to the local Con Ed office on Pitkin Avenue, Brooklyn, with $0.50 a week to pay for them. All was recorded in a small receipt book with stamps indicating payment received.

Following is a story I related to each of my children as they grew up.

As an infant, my sister Selma developed asthma, necessitating a weekly injection by a Manhattan specialist. Four dollars a visit! Mama would take the train Saturday morning into Manhattan and leave me with $0.40 for my day's expenses. For lunch after synagogue I'd visit the local kosher deli for a pastrami sandwich – $0.15, potato salad dish – $0.05, bottle of soda – $0.05. Next, a double feature movie with endless cartoons and short subjects (a five hour event) – $0.10. I'd exhaust my allowance with a candy bar – $0.05.

Yes, everything was cheap, but people were penniless during the Depression Years.

THE WATCH

For my Bar Mitzvah, among some minor gifts, Papa presented me with a genuine 14K gold-plated Bulova watch. Needless to say, its worth far exceeded in value all my other possessions. As a result (as per tradition), it was never worn, except on special occasions, of which I can't remember any.

2½ years later the accident occurred.

I was assisting in the Bookkeeping Dept. at Commerce High School, a perk for good students during study periods. I was an "A" student in bookkeeping – in those days I was considered very smart – when a Mr. Hamburg called on us one day. He was an alumnus of Commerce High. It was the height of WW II, 1943, and Mr. H needed junior accountants for his small accounting firm, really bookkeepers to do write-ups at his various clients throughout the City. He asked me (as office manager) to suggest two outstanding students. Naturally, I chose myself and a certain John Logan, also of our office.

We were hired on the spot at $0.35 an hour. I was 15½ and the aforementioned Mr. Logan 17½.

On my first day at work, Mr. H advised me the position had three prerequisites:

1. Always enter a client's office wearing a jacket (as a professional).
2. Never walk in without a briefcase or manila envelope in your hand. He gave me $0.25 to buy a manila envelope.
3. You must have a watch to keep track of your hours at 0.35 per.

The rest is history and painful at that, since the only watch I had was the Bulova.

When I informed dear Dad that I would need to take the Bulova to work at $0.35 an hour, smoke came out of his ears. But the watch was mine and this was a career stepping-stone. Disaster was inevitable; within a month the wristband made of genuine gold-plated links, was bent in an accident. The only one I could confide this information to was Mama; a repair was secretly made.

In the midst of my employment, Mr. Hamburg decided "to get with it" and changed his name to Hilton. I'm sure the daily bombing of Hamburg, Germany during WWII was also a factor. I never adjusted to the new moniker, but the incident still remains with me 50 plus years after.

Jerry Mink, the Bar Mitzvah boy, August 1940

THE ROLL

As the months rolled by and my salary remained constant, my hope of becoming a professional accountant withered under the torment of adding long columns of figures. According to Mr. Hilton, "Accountant's do not use adding machines!" so my dream faltered under the drudgery.

One day Hilton called me at one of the clients. "Mr. Mink, we are all celebrating Mr. Logan's 18th birthday tomorrow with a luncheon. Join us at the famous Down Under (Australian motif) Restaurant located at the lower levels of Rockefeller Center at 1 p.m. promptly." What a perk! My experiences of eating "out" with my family at a midtown high-class restaurant were nil.

Needless to say, at 1 p.m. I was at the Down Under to join my two colleagues. Naturally, I was carrying my manila envelope, which at this point was laden with old newspapers so it wouldn't flop in the wind.

I was handed a menu, studied it, got the drift of their price range, and ordered something priced in-between – a bowl of bean soup, a Down Under specialty.

Waiting to be served and being absorbed in the professional small talk, I took a knife – as we did at home – and started to cut across my roll, in order to butter it entirely in one shmear. At this point, Mr. Hilton brought me up short. "Mr. Mink, we accountants don't butter our rolls by opening them up. Rather we tear off a section like this." My embarrassment was catastrophic. But we continued the celebration of John's birthday with a slice each of Down Under's famous cheesecake. Some months later, I went back to helping Papa at the Junk

Shop. (No other help was available during the war.) Hilton and Logan pursued the accounting profession with great success, I hope, though Price, Waterhouse and Arthur Anderson were never threatened, I'm certain.

It has been 50+ years, but each time I am at a restaurant and served a roll I relive that trauma.

PAPA'S JUNK SHOP

As best as I can remember, Papa began his business career as an apprentice to a junk peddler – a distant relation – Mr. Slavin – on a horse-and-wagon – in, of all places, Watertown, NY. Buying and trading metal scrap for household implements and tools and sometimes, cash. As a sideline, they also bought fur skins from the farmers. They would leave every Monday morning (as related by Papa) and return Friday with scrap, furs, and what have you, to sell on the local market. World War I and the call-up; Pop was drafted. He got as far as Alabama; something to do with maintaining the Army's horses and jackasses, a hidden facility he never thereafter employed. Upon his discharge, with his separation payout and monies he had made playing cards, he went into partnership with his brother-in-law, a picturesque character, Sam Krupnick! Sam K, who had married Papa's sister, Rachel, was a Sharpy, with an eye for the ladies. As Papa told it, Sam's talents lay in two areas; the first was taking big risks. For example, they would buy a load of scrap, spend a week preparing the material for shipment – weighing, sorting, packing, etc. At the point where the final accounting was established, Sam would suggest he and the seller play a hand of poker, double or nothing, and ofttimes he found someone of a like interest. So it was boom or bust alternately.

The second talent was Sam K's attention to the opposite sex. At some point, he met a rich widow, took off for California with her and left poor Aunt Rachel with two young children, penniless and pitiful. Yes, Sam was a real character, but not a decent one. (I met him many years later on a visit to California.)

Papa, two months before his demise in 1957, known as Little Hymie, Mr. Cards

Papa had no other choice but to continue the junk business alone. About this time, he had married Mama and began doing business somewhat successfully, but got involved in a practice of shipping copper scrap to Phelps Dodge, in Laurel Hills, NY, without pricing. This scheme appealed to his gambling instinct. Of course, the copper market could only go up! Right? Wrong! The Depression hit him hard, copper prices, like everything else, collapsed, and Pop was broke.

Some months later, Aunt Sonia, his sister, loaned him about $800 – a fortune in those days – and he started up again in Corona, Queens, NY. At that point, most of the garbage in Brooklyn and Queens was deposited in the Corona dump (subsequently renamed Fresh Meadows). In a scene now replayed in Third World countries, grown men and children would scour the garbage looking for metal scrap and other recyclables. Papa opened a scrap metal shop to buy up these daily pickings, and was surprisingly successful. But his obsessive card playing with his Italian cronies occupied much of the afternoon and early evenings. Eventually the site became the home for the first and second NY World Fairs. The World Fair authorities forced him to move to another location in Corona, which was to witness the end of his business career and his life cycle 20 years later.

AUNT DOTTY AND THE 30'S CLASS DISTINCTIONS

On reflection, the 20s and 30s were truly another world. When Mama and Aunt Dotty arrived in America in 1921, they moved into the home of their Aunt Gussy Segal in Williamsburg, Brooklyn. Single girls *did not* live alone for reasons of modesty. Secondly, every dollar they could scrape together, they would send back to their penniless family in Bialystok, to assist their parents and five younger siblings.

Mama was 20 and Dotty 18 on arrival. Gussy had several children; I can recall only Fanny and Abe. Unlike Uncle Dovid, Gussy prodded her children to acquire a college education. Fanny went to university and there met and married Dr. Miller. (Personages of high professional achievement were never referred to by first name.)

Dr. Miller was a highly respected physician – Ear, Nose and Throat – associated with Beth Israel Hospital in lower Manhattan. Thereafter, anyone in the family with serious medical problems went to Dr. Miller. (Free of charge, I believe.) The entire family extended him and Fanny great respect. In fact, when his name was mentioned, there was always a discernible adjustment in vocal resonance. The Miller family resided in a brownstone in lower Manhattan and were obviously several strata of social significance above the greenhorns. They had two daughters. It should be made known in passing that Uncle Dovid's younger daughter, Ruthie, who developed brain cancer, was successfully operated on by the world-reknowned surgeon, Dr. Leon Davidoff (see Encyclopedia Judaica) without a fee, as a professional courtesy to Dr. Miller.

But that is not this story.

All Mama's family were handsome people. Aunt Dotty and Abe Segal were first cousins living in the same apartment and fell in love. But Aunt Gussy would have none of that. First of all, they were first cousins. Secondly, and much more serious, Dotty was a greenhorn with no formal education, whereas her son, Abe, was a professional accountant – a totally different social level. Aunt Gussy, a powerful woman as I recall, had her way. A disappointed Abe was provided with a shidduch; an American young lady who unfortunately died at an early age, after presenting Abe with two children. Eventually, he married again, to a widow. I don't recall Abe ever looking happy. My dear Aunt Dotty was heartsick, yet still attractive. So, in my opinion, "dafka" to spite Gussy, she married the only college graduate she probably knew, the local pharmacist, Uncle George Mann, who thereafter was captivated and forever in love with Dotty. They had a problematic marriage; Dotty remained childless and they were separated for perhaps five to seven years. Dotty became successful as a dressmaker (Mama called her "golden hands"). She had her own business, couturiere to wealthy society women.

George remained a pharmacist and insurance salesman and waited for Dotty to return to their marriage. She eventually did. They lived comfortably and in the end my dear Aunt Dotty suffered with Alzheimer's. George tended her at home for years, till she passed on in her late 70's. I'll always remember the dedicated Uncle George Mann saying, all he wished for himself was to live one day more than Dotty so he could take care of her to the end.

And so it happened. He passed on quietly several months after Aunt Dotty.

COMMERCE HIGH SCHOOL
MANHATTAN NYC

In the 1930-40's, high school education in New York City was divided into neighborhood high schools and a group of specialty schools. Brooklyn Tech for engineering, Stuyvesant for high average students, Music and Art – self evident, and Haaren High School for metal and aviation trades. For the creme de la creme of academia, Townsand Harris or Bronx Science. Charles J. Mink chose Commerce High in midtown Manhattan, two train rides from Jackson Heights, about one hour each way.

Why Commerce? As I explained, my father operated a small junk shop without *any* formal education, as did his cronies, mostly all greenhorns. They were hard workers, survivors, with the ability to turn a dollar, but lacking in record keeping, reading or arithmetic skills. Amazing, but some of them ran businesses employing dozens of workers, especially in the needle trades, and they prospered.

What was their secret? Find an "American" educated bookkeeper or accountant to keep records for the authorities!

Papa's expert was *Mr. Sam Shapiro*. He spoke well, with authority, always wore a jacket and a tie, kept everything in order and was highly respected for his acumen in English reading and writing by the community of immigrant businessmen. He was a certified accountant and lived well, all traits I admired.

So whom should I wish to emulate and so as to gain my father's respect and koved[1] and also that of his clan of cronies? I would become another Sam

---

1. koved – honor, respect.

Shapiro. Fortunately, I had some good innate skills: always very good in arithmetic and mathematics, poor in languages, until today. I had well above average marks in grade school; I skipped twice and graduated high school at 16. (At that time, above average students were pushed forward.) So looking through the catalogues of high schools available in the City system, I found that Commerce High School on West 66th Street in Manhattan stood out: "Preparation for pursuing a business career and attaining a degree in accounting at the university level."

I applied, and with my grade score I was readily accepted.

As one entered the building, one thing stood out: a huge athletic trophy case. The centerpiece was our claim to fame; we were the high school of Lou Gehrig, with pictures and numerous trophies of our championship baseball teams.

Since we were in Manhattan in the 30's, some black boys from Harlem also filtered through, which resulted in our having a crack city track team.

I became an "A" student in bookkeeping and accounting, which led to my being chosen to assist during study periods in the Bookkeeping Department Office. Hence I met the previously mentioned Mr. Hamburg a.k.a. Mr. Hilton, and there followed my decision not to follow in Mr. Shapiro's footsteps. When I finally became a businessman, Mr. Sam Shapiro was my accountant of record for several years. We parted after I discovered he had limited talents and some questionable practices, but that's loshen hora[1] and forbidden.

---

1. loshen hora – saying bad things (literally evil tongue).

DAD, THE CARD PLAYER

Whenever I retrace my life with Papa and our relationship, there are several pictures I quickly recapture.

1. Working with or for him in the junk shop. He always left for the shop at 7:15 a.m., even after playing cards into the early hours of the morning. But that did not disturb him since he went to sleep at his desk as soon as he got to work.
2. Standing over his right shoulder as he played cards. You name it, gin rummy, pinochle, poker – five or seven cards. I was a witness to it all.

Was he a good player? He should have been after 40 plus years playing. I'd say he depended more on luck than scientific evaluations or skill. One thing is for certain. He was not a good loser, a scenario I was privy to on many occasions. When Papa was playing poker and had an opening hand of three kings, e.g., betting heavily against all upcomers, if someone would buy a straight or flush on the last card, to take the pot, in his anger, he would take the three kings and rip them up. Needless to say, the other players would erupt into a screaming match since they now needed a new deck. "This is it! We can't play with you any more, Mink." Of course it was an invalid oath. For within five minutes all was forgotten as the repetitive and boring repartee of the regular players would continue. The dealer called out two fives, three clubs, possible straight, etc., etc., etc... and so it went on, as little Jerry Mink watched.

Postscript on Papa

Most of my early memories of Papa were when he saw me and he'd call out, "Jerry, get me a pack of Luckies, Camels, Old Gold, etc."

He would continually change brands when his cigarette cough got heavy. He would never think to stop smoking, but rather scream, "Damn Luckies, Camel, Old Gold," which was usually followed by a brand change.

The day *after* his first heart attack, he never smoked another cigarette again.

MINK, THE MARINER

I assume during the wars here in Israel the young men had similar experiences. By 1945, every able-bodied man from 17-40 was inducted or volunteered in the US armed forces.

America, a nation of 135,000,000 at that stage, was at total war. The newspapers were filled with war news and daily lists of casualties; Hollywood films were all war oriented; the radio had continuous war related reports or analysis. Almost my entire high school graduation class promptly entered the armed services. (Remember, I graduated at 16.) I applied to and entered a sparsely populated NYU School of Commerce, pursuing a degree in accounting (as described in an earlier chapter). Would you believe a tuition of $240.00 per semester, with a school-sponsored outlet selling used books, costing a total of $60-$70 per year.

My friends had all entered the services. The street corners and youth clubs were devoid of men, except for the occasional returning soldier. I recall joining the C.A.P. (Civil Air Patrol), and was supplied a uniform. The purpose (for me) was not to become a pilot; rather I wished to be less conspicuous, with a military appearing uniform to wear when not at school. We did march around a bit, saluted, and played soldier a few nights a month.

For some reason the Navy appealed to me: it was cleaner. The pictures of soldiers showed them grimy and worn out; not for Jerry Mink. After completing two semesters of university, I enlisted at 17½ and was relieved finally to be a part of the war effort.

I won't bore you with the stories of a sheltered, nice Jewish boy now thrown in with 100 men from totally different backgrounds. It's the same in every army, but one episode sticks out.

Place many young men together and there are always games, horseplay, you name it. This idiot chose a huge corn-fed farm boy to play a trick on. Why? I knew he could never catch me in a race. After the stunt, where someone pushed him over my crouched body, he began chasing me. As we rounded a corner, we ran into an officer.

Officer: "What's going on here?"

JM: "We were kidding around, Sir."

Farm boy: "I'm trying to get even with him, sir."

Officer: "This is not the way sailors get even. Wednesday night, at the 'Smoker,' you can have it out like sailors, in the ring, not by chasing around like kids."

Mink, the Mariner, US Navy

To be honest, I was really scared to get into the ring with this Goliath. What did I really know about boxing? My friends began giving me intensive boxing instructions. I did not want to appear yellow, but I weighed in at 155 pounds and stood 5'10". "Goliath" was at least 220 pounds, 6'3". Wednesday night arrived; I watched the other matches and was preparing for the beating of my life. The referee, Steve Bellois, was a former high-ranked professional fighter. We wore our swim trunks and t-shirts, sneakers and boxing gloves. Finally, our turn. I was sweating and nervous. We climbed into the ring. The referee looked at us and saved my life. "A light middleweight vs. a heavyweight? – no match." Another case of D.I., I'm certain.

After boot camp at Samson Training Station, NY, we were given the standard tests for evaluating our capabilities, and then interviewed. The officer in charge: "Seaman Mink, you have unusually high arithmetic and math skills. I'm sure the Navy will find a special place for you." I observed my entire company divided and shipped off for special training and schooling. Seaman Mink sat around week after week. No assignment. My imagination was exploding. Where would Uncle Sam send me? Finally, The Day. Posted on a single large assignment sheet, my name alone. *Special Assignment* – Norfolk, VA, headquarters of the Atlantic Fleet, *no less*. I took my sealed orders and train tickets, and concluded this must be a choice position. On arrival in Norfolk, I reported again to a Placement Officer. I was directed to the Officers' Quarters. I was assigned to the Transit Officers Dining Hall to sell meal tickets at $0.35 for breakfast; $0.50 for lunch and dinner. Sunday special dinner was $0.75 for guests of the officers; and of course, at night, movie theater tickets at $0.25. For this special assignment, the Navy had chosen the creme de la creme, this arithmetic and math super achiever.

Month after dreary month passed. Was this going to be my contribution to the war effort? I became friendly with some of the officers passing through, including a Wave officer (woman sailor). I appealed to her that I wanted to go to sea. This was not the Navy I had dreamed of. One day, a new aircraft carrier, Tarawa CV40, docked. I implored her to assign me to sea duty on this ship. By this point, I had a back-up ticket seller. I got my wish.

On reporting aboard, again a review of my abilities. Yes, we can use you in the storeroom, about 10 levels below deck. Someone had to count and keep records of the food supplies. However, at general quarters (for battle), I was assigned as a twin 20MM anti-aircraft gunner.

The war was quickly approaching a crescendo; Germany had surrendered. The Tarawa was preparing for the next major battle in the Pacific in a tactic of step-by-step defeat of the Japanese via island hopping, with the invasion of Truk, the Imperial Japanese Navy's main base. Armaments were being loaded day and night for this epic confrontation. Now, 1st Class Seaman Mink *again* was busy counting, this time the incoming armaments. At this point the A-Bomb was exploded. The War was over. My mother, z"l,[1] wrote, "You were always lucky." It meant I would not have to risk my life.

After loading up for a few weeks, we finally went to sea. I now had a new, horrible assignment: food server – called in the Navy a mess cook. I was up at 4:30 am, serving with a group of other seamen, the 2,000 men, three times a day. Endless drudgery: serve, clean up, serve, clean up. It was the pits. I again was very depressed. Again, this was not the Navy of my dreams. Lying on my canvas cot, resting between meals one afternoon, I heard an officer call out, "Can any of you *animals* type?" I jumped up and explained I was probably the best typist they'll ever find (thanks to Commerce High School). The remainder of my shipboard service was a vacation by comparison: typing up reports, plans of the day and activities.

After some six months at sea, an announcement: the ship was going to the Far East for extended duty. Those who did not wish to re-enlist would be sent home for discharge. I sent a letter to NYU announcing my return for studies and came home to Mama's tender care and my own bed.

But a lot wiser, with many lasting memories and experiences.

---

1. z"l – to be rememberd with a blessing.

MY UNCLE GEORGE
AND THE EARLY YEARS

The pattern was, first Papa came to the States without a trade, around 1910, and went to work as an apprentice to the Slavin family of Watertown, NY, distant relatives, as a junkman's helper. Some 20 years later, Mama's younger brother, George, came to the States, thanks again to Aunt Alexander, also without a trade and went to work for Papa in the Corona (Fresh Meadows) junk shop. He eventually left some years later to start off on his own, after marrying Aunt Edith. Now with a trade, he went to work for Albert Brothers, a large, successful business in Waterbury, Conn. Some 10 years later, George began his own business in New Haven, Conn., and finally, in Albany, NY.

I had completed about three years toward my B.A. at NYU, but with the passing of Mama (my educational driving force), I quit school, bought a fifth hand small pick-up truck and began buying and picking up scrap iron and batteries, etc., mostly at gas stations and repair shops.

Amazingly, I was 21 and earning more than any of my peers, over $100/week in 1949. Remember, at that time one could buy a new home in Long Island for $3,400.

The down side was that being a junkman lacked charisma. Imagine meeting a nice Jewish girl and she inquired as to what I do. Do I answer, "I'm a junkman!"? Really no "tam."[1] So I sold the truck (out of shame) and took a job as assistant bookkeeper at Park Square Lumber in Brooklyn, NY. Park Square Lumber was Parker and Savadorf, two go-go Jewish boys who were in the right

---

1. tam – proper taste or effect.

business at the right time. The suburbs were being built (via G.I. loans), family homes were springing up like mushrooms, and I grabbed this "respectable" position for $35 a week. Now, when asked what I did, I could reply, "I'm in the lumber business." In retrospect, it all sounds like madness, but totally true, nevertheless.

THE YOUNG BUCK

I worked at Park Square Lumber for about a year. I then met a nice Jewish girl in Asbury Park, the Mink family summer habitat, and fell in love, probably more with her mother's kindness and concern for me than with her 19-year old daughter. I was 21 and Mama had died two years ago. I desperately needed to fill that void in my life.

I asked Mayda Twersky for her hand in marriage. I bought a ring for $1,000 – (a great deal of money at that point. A new car sold for under $2,000) – earned from my junk business days. The shidduch was ill-advised. We broke the engagement after six months by mutual accord. Note: Papa was mad when I got engaged and irate when we broke up. He had presented us with a set of sterling silver cutlery for $350. Papa: "Every time you make a move it costs me money!" The Twerskys had kept all the engagement gifts "to cover their expenses." I did get back the ring. The Twersky engagement was probably doomed when Mr. Twersky insisted that as an engaged man I now had to buy and wear a fedora. Well, I bought one, carried it around in a paper bag and wore it only on entering their home. When I first resisted buying it, Mr. T insisted, saying, "That's the way it's done." This phrase would haunt me on many other occasions.

The following summer, the Korean War was heating up and the newspapers told of ex-servicemen being called up again. (Who knows, there might be a shortage of Navy anti-aircraft gunners who could type. I was *very* versatile. Covered in the chapter on Mink, the Mariner.)

In reality it was like all wars, dreadful, since about 4,000,000 Koreans, North and South, were killed – with Chinese intervention – in the war. Plus

33,600 American soldiers, as they battled up and down the Korean peninsula. What was it all about? A decision to stop Communism, the socialist experiment in government that died 40 years later from its own ineptitude and false premises.

So Jerry and his pal Curt Lowenthal drove down to Asbury Park (again) for a last fling before possibly being called up, which never happened. Instead, I met Gloria Stamberg, a moderately attractive woman my age. She had been a good student, graduated from Rutgers University and was employed in a Manhattan office. We dated for a few months, and one night, driving from her home in Jersey City, I nearly got killed, having fallen asleep at the wheel. A decision had to be made: get married or discontinue the affair. Remember, a ring was available. The situation at home was untenable. We were both working. So why not?

In retrospect, the smart move should have been to take a room somewhere. I wasn't earning enough at Park Square for an apartment and I was only 22. But, remember, it's 1950 and the modus operandi for single Jewish men and women was to live at home till they married.

By this point, I had reached the $45 a week level, having started at $35 (in a year). I also came to the conclusion that if I intended to learn the lumber business, it would have to be in the yard and not shuffling invoices in the office. The bosses agreed and gave me an additional $5 raise to $50, with the promise of more to come. To my chagrin, I also quickly realized how much money was being made, having seen the purchase and sales prices and now the physical expediting of the business. Not to mention that specified grade marked lumber was being mixed and sold with ungraded stock (a scam). Remember, I was always good at numbers and here I was making $50 a week as yard shipping manager; what chutzpah – I was getting less than any of the unionized shleppers, and they – the bosses – were becoming millionaires.

Following the wedding and a honeymoon in Miami and Cuba, I had driven down in my new Studebaker Commander (top of the line – $2,100) again, bought with money from my earlier junk business days. I walked into the offices of the bosses at Park Square. "Gentlemen, I can't make it on $50 a week." Jack Parker, who was really the powerhouse of this operation, replied, "Jerry, as soon as I return from my Florida vacation, we'll review the entire situation." Jack left that day. Next morning I entered the office of his partner, Abe Savadorf, and quit.

Abe: "You can't do that!"

Jerry: "How important can I be at $50 a week?"

Well, now I was married and jobless. I returned to Papa's scrap yard, announced I was no longer a lumber man and asked what kind of deal we could work out, with an eventual partnership down the road. Papa's response? I still hear ringing in my ears. "Are you mishuga (crazy)? But now that you're married you can always hang around here at $75 a week." Shaken but not totally surprised, I answered, "I think I'll hang around somewhere else." That was the extent of Papa's largesse. Next week I withdrew $700 I had saved from wedding presents and bought another fifth hand GMC truck.

The first week's peddling I earned $127 – loading scrap iron by hand at the salvage yard of Merit Metal Smelting in the Bronx, owned by Micha Klein. Mr. Klein was a friend, and recognizing I needed a start, he gave me a chance to earn a week's pay. I never looked back.

In retrospect, Papa's job offer was the best thing he ever did for me in business. I learned to survive. As my new-found friend, Mike Kramer, says, "There's no free lunch."

I resolved then and there to be proud of whatever I had to do, even if it meant being called a junk man, as long as I had a jingle in my pocket.

MY FIRST FORAY
INTO POLITICS

Adlai Stevenson

The elegance, candor, intellect and unpretentious personality of Mr. Stevenson, the Democratic presidential candidate in 1952, captured my youthful enthusiasm. I became frustrated sitting in front of the tube. We were then living in a rented apartment in Jackson Heights, a perk from my Park Square Lumberyard days, since the owners had contacts with many of the major builders. At that time, it was nearly impossible to find an available rental apartment. A matter of supply not meeting demand after World War II. Back to my saga.

I soon found the local Stevenson campaign headquarters, in a temporarily rented store front. I asked those in charge what I could do to help get Stevenson elected. There ensued endless nights of canvassing on the streets, knocking on apartment house doors, etc. One evening, our local chairman suggested I go out and speak on an open sound-truck with a driver and American flag. We were assigned to a right-wing German American neighborhood, Richmond Hill in Queens, NY, predominantly a blue collar area. You have to remember that Adlai was opposed by the national hero, Ike.

This very inept public orator (see chapter on Dale Carnegie) was delivered like a korbon (sacrificial lamb) to the train station as people returned home after a long day at work. The set presentation was simple: "Remember what the Roosevelt and Truman eras had done to establish social justice in America," etc. I obviously was not getting my message across to the small crowd. I was the wrong speaker in the wrong venue. Suddenly, I was besieged by hecklers, "Go home, you Commie," with other such invectives arriving often, in addition to catcalls. Finally, a ripe tomato splattered the side of the truck and splashed on yours truly. Always quick with a response, I called out, "Are you throwing the rotten fruit at me or the flag?" With this, the crowd began to surge forward. I banged on the hood of the truck; luckily, the driver was at the wheel and had the motor running – to charge the batteries for the loudspeaker. I yelled, "Let's get the hell out of here before these Germans kill another Jew!"

The epilogue is history; Stevenson was overwhelmed and defeated.

Jerry Mink, the Representative

Shortly after the campaign we were called together by the local Democratic party for a farewell and thank you gathering. At this juncture in the political history of New York State, the liberal elements were divided into two entities: the regular national Democratic Party and a labor-oriented group, the New York Liberal Party. The latter was financed by the ILGWU (International Ladies Garment Workers Union), a Jewish organization from floor to ceiling, including, of course, most of the garment workers. (How the world has changed in 50 years!) Then the garment workers were Jewish, Italian and Polish immigrants. Now, garments are produced in the Far East. The Queens County leader and political powerhouse in the Liberal Party was a Mr. Davidson. He approached me at the event.

Mr. D.: "Mr. Mink (remember I was 25 at the time), I have been watching you during the campaign. I'm impressed by your enthusiasm. Our organization is still very weak in Queens County. (Few garment workers lived there, plus a small Jewish population then. The Jews resided mostly in the Bronx and Brooklyn.) We have practically no organization in Jackson Heights. As Queens County chairman, and co-chairman of the Liberal Party in New York City, I have the authority to offer you the position of Jackson Heights representative to the Queens council of the Liberal Party." (Quite a feather in the cap for the kid!) I was quite flattered and accepted on the spot.

Within a month, I was notified by mail of my first Queens County Council meeting and introduced by Mr. Davidson to the assembly. We then began the business of the meeting, various reports, etc. All very boring. As the meeting ended, Davidson arose. "Although our presidential candidate, Mr. Stevenson, was defeated, on the local level, as you know, we co-supported with the Democrats Mr. X as US Congressman from Queens County (applause). As reward for our efforts, we have been granted the opportunity to appoint one of the aides for the new Congressman in Washington. I'd like to nominate Mr. Y for that postion. Is there a seconder for the motion?"

(Almost unanimous.)

Who should arise to address the assembly? The new boy from Jackson Heights, yours truly.

JM: "Mr. Chairman, I'd like to know more about Mr. Y before I cast my vote."

Davidson: "Mr. Mink, I suggest you give yourself time to work into the organization, get to know the people and the system."

Jerry Mink abstained, resigned his Representative position in embarrassment, and never attended another meeting. This was not the Democratic system I had espoused as a Stevenson ideologue.

THE FAMILY

After Mama's passing, my sister Selma, 4½ years my junior, and I were basically left to fend for ourselves emotionally. After a few months, Papa went back to his old ways, played cards several evenings a week plus weekends. That was his lifestyle, *period*. But he did maintain the home with a housekeeper for some years. About three years after my marriage to Gloria (which was primarily to get out of the house, as explained previously), our Uncle George Gering and his wife, Edith, took Selma for a vacation to the Catskills. Selma had graduated with a B.A. in secretarial studies from NYU and was employed in a New York City office.

In reality, they wanted her to meet some eligible young men. However, she and the waiter at their table, Arty Lubkin (a law student), became enamored. They eventually married and settled in Brooklyn. In time, they purchased a home on Long Island and raised three sons. Arty pursued a legal career for 35 years and is now semi-retired. Approximately 10 years ago, he even ventured into the field of politics, basically a non-starter, as a Democrat in solidly Republican Nassau County, LI, NY.

Almost eight years after Mama's passing, Papa suddenly announced he was getting married. He had been living alone. His social contacts continued to be his card game pals, it was reasonable he should not live alone. But when we met Paulie *after* the marriage, it was a cause of consternation for the family. I didn't really care. He was a sick man, having suffered two heart attacks plus diabetes, and the residual effects of 40 years smoking. Plus, he was the type that never maintained good health habits. We also called her Paulie (Papa couldn't pronounce Pauline). The contrast was outrageous:

1. Papa stood 5'2". He could never buy a ready-made suit. Paulie was at least 5'10".
2. Papa weighed about 140 pounds. He was stocky and powerful; I know this from the times he let me have it. Paulie outweighed him by at least 40-50 pounds.
3. Pop was 66 (or 68) years old, and Paulie 42-44 and once divorced.
4. Pop could not read, write or properly sign his name. She was an American, an educated woman who was formerly employed in a civil service job.

But they did have one common denominator – her family was in the scrap business in Asbury Park, NJ.

Within a year or so, Papa passed away during a cancer operation. A new monster arose: The Will and the Legal Rights of the bereaved widow.

THE CADILLAC RAFFLE OCEANSIDE LI, NY JEWISH CENTER

1953. I was all of 26, married, with our baby, Lisa, and still working off a truck, with a small one-car garage for storage. But I was already the owner of a mortgage-free home in Oceanside, Long Island, a new car, and obviously doing well. The split-level house had cost about $20,000, average for that time.

Upon arriving in the community we did the same as many other Jewish couples: we joined the local Jewish Center and immediately became active. In a year or two I was membership chairman and on the board of trustees of the shul and Men's Club.

As is the case in most Jewish centers, there were two groups – pro and anti the rabbi (Eliyahu Kasten). For several years I was "parve" (neutral). But an unpredictable event occurred. There was a synagogue raffle and a mix-up in tickets. (The prize was a new Cadillac, believe it or not, or $5,000 cash). The rabbi drew the winning ticket, and the wrong number was called the winner, a very complex situation. Accusations flew which were grist for the pro- and anti-rabbi forces who felt it was not handled properly. J.M. now joined the anti-rabbi forces.

I called a meeting of the anti group in my home, with the purpose of organizing a campaign, since the rabbi's contract was coming up for renewal in a few months. I was defined as "The Kid On the Block" since there were many professionals (lawyers, doctors, and successful businessmen), and I was just a blue-collar junkman.

The night of the general meeting arrived. My friend, pro-rabbi attorney David Brecker (then president), called the meeting to order. There must have been 600-700 people in the packed shul auditorium. As the meeting was brought to order, who should enter the meeting hall? None other than but Rabbi Kasten. He sat down on the stage, facing the congregation. The silence was electrifying.

Brecker: "Rabbi, welcome to the meeting, but I'm surprised at your presence."

Rabbi: "I'm aware there is a smear campaign going on and I will not allow another McCarthy type forum (vintage 1950's)."

Brecker: "Any objections to the rabbi's presence?"

Silence.

Brecker: "The first order of business is the renewal of the rabbi's contract. Who wishes to speak pro?" Naturally several members of the pro-rabbi group rose, praised the rabbi profusely and offered a motion to extend the contract for an additional three years.

Brecker: "Anyone opposed?"

I looked around the room. All the stalwarts of the opposition had collapsed in silence. I couldn't believe it. After years of dissatisfaction and verbal attacks, not one anti speaker. I guess you know what happened; yours truly arose before the hushed assemblage, unprepared, never having spoken to more than 10 people at one time. My mind and thoughts were in total disarray. Today, I still don't know what I said. The rabbi's contract was renewed.

What I do remember are any number of people congratulating me, not on my presentation but rather, my chutzpah. That basically was the conclusion of my Oceanside Jewish Center shul activity. We moved out of the community several years later to East Hills, in Roslyn, NY. I did not become a shul activist in that community.

P.S. At the end of the next three year period, Rabbi Kasten's contract was *not* renewed.

DALE CARNEGIE

Several months after Rabbi Kasten's reelection I hired a contractor to do some work at my home. Surprisingly, he met up with another craftsman and they greeted each other like old friends. They had been classmates at a Dale Carnegie Course given on Long Island.

I was impressed by their relationship and made inquiries. They had been enrolled in this course and regaled me with details about its results. I soon started a series of 16 lessons, at about $20.00 per session. This was the '60s and $20 was real money. The O.J.C. debate taught me I lacked public speaking skills and self-confidence.

The series of lessons was to become useful on future occasions when I had to get up on my feet and express myself. I still employ the basic course material today. The watchwords were: "All people have butterflies in their stomach when they rise to speak to an audience. Dale Carnegie teaches you to keep them flying in formation." I also prize highly the two green mechanical pencils I won for best presentation at two sessions.

THE WILL
or
GREED SHOWS ITS UGLY COUNTENANCE

It's true I have worked to make money from the age of 12, at times collecting waste paper, or as a delivery boy, a junior accountant, in the lumber business, or working in Papa's junkyard for tuition for university. After my service, I came under the G.I. Bill, and had my own scrap business. You name it, I've probably done it – yes, for money.

I admire wealth and those who have accumulated it, and the fact that it has afforded me a good, comfortable lifestyle most of my adult years. What really overwhelms me are the lengths people are willing to venture to lay their hands on money.

The Pauline Saga

As stated before, I had little to do with Papa's second marriage and was completely "parve" (neutral) on the matter.

When Papa's final ailment (the cancer operation) occurred, I was helping to manage in his small junk business, which over the years had really deteriorated, plus doing my own trading, basically off a truck. On the morning of the fateful operation, I sat in the visitors' room of Memorial Hospital in Flushing, Queens. *Alone*. Surprisingly, Pauline was absent.

Several hours passed, and eventually the operating surgeon came down solemn-faced. Papa had died of a heart seizure during the massive procedure to remove the cancerous colon section. Immediately, I called all the concerned parties from a pay phone. Still no Pauline – in the hospital or at home, either.

It was eventually discovered that while I was sitting in the hospital, she was sitting at a lawyer's office to program her actions in the event of Papa's demise. As the widow, she called the hospital from the outside, and on learning of his passing, promptly went to his bank, froze his accounts, safe deposit box, etc., and sent letters to anyone that she knew owed him money. I had gone to the funeral director to arrange burial for the following day, unaware of all the action taking place behind the scenes. I can still recall the funeral: friends and family were solemn; Papa was not a really lovable character. But the two that wailed and sobbed the loudest were Pauline and *her sister*!

I must insert at this point that Papa was considered a wealthy man – far, far beyond its reality. Why? Number one, because he was in business for 35 or more years, and two, he never spent money.

After rising from sitting shiva, I returned to Papa's place (the shop), and discovered Pauline – who somehow had a set of keys – with her brother, taking inventory in the scrapyard. Remember, her family were scrap dealers also. I called at the bank. I had to pay many immediate expenses. Several years earlier, I was given power of attorney to sign company checks, since Papa was often ailing and had begun going on vacations following his marriage to Paulie. The bank manager, Mr. Larkin, an old friend from my air raid warden days, told me that the day Papa had died, he was presented with a court order freezing all accounts and transactions of the deceased.

I had no choice; I put my own money into a new account, received a sizable advance from another scrap dealer who trusted me, and resumed our businesses, in unison. The next act was the climactic scene at the bank when the safe deposit box was opened in the presence of a NY State representative, Pauline, the grieving widow in black, of course, my sister and myself. Pauline's brother was also there, as advisor, and sat outside. In the safe was a small amount of cash, some miscellaneous papers and *The Will*.

The State Tax Authority took inventory first and then began the reading of the will. On hearing that there was no question about her being the widow with legal one third ownership of the estate, the bereaved widow leapt to her feet, ran to the other room, and shouted to her brother, *"Al, it's good, it's good!"* That unforgettable scene is still etched in my mind as if were today.

Final Act: The Will is Executed.

It's pathetic, but the will was very poorly drawn up. My father had employed an attorney whom he paid $75 to draw up the document. The attorney was eventually disbarred. Papa could lose a few hundred dollars at a card game, but to make his will he only spent $75, that was my Pop. My brother-in-law, having recently graduated from law school, became involved with evaluating the contents and real intentions of Papa. Basically, the will had five articles:

1. Sister Selma received a set amount which radically improved her life style. The Lubkins bought a home on Long Island and sundries.
2. A minor amount for charity, no delineation.
3. Pauline was the widow.
4. I got the business, whatever that meant.
5. There were three executors named:
   1. Myself.
   2. Julius Reinlieb, a cousin by marriage, an established attorney.
   3. Abe Mink, a mildly successful clothing manufacturer and Papa's first cousin.

Promptly, Abe phoned. He was too busy to become an executor, and resigned. About a year later, we met at a social function. Abe told me he now was sorry he resigned. He could have earned some money as executor, and *maybe* that was his dear cousin's (Papa's) way of including him as an heir. (No comment.)

At a subsequent meeting with Pauline and her brother, they were enlightened: she was entitled to *the income* of one third of the estate (not cash) and as executors, we could invest it in 1% NYS 50-year bonds, totally legal, earning her $700 a year, at most. Net result, we settled giving Pauline $25,000, and as a bonus, ownership of Papa's used Cadillac (which she had gotten accustomed to driving!!) She drove away with the check and her car, never to be heard from again.

I continued to run the business. After paying off various State, Federal and inheritance taxes and sundry debts, I inherited a used truck, but, at last, a place to do business. This took me off the truck as a junkman; I was now a scrap dealer.

HOW COULD ANYONE GET MARRIED FIVE TIMES? GLORIA, WIFE #1

This is my basic response: Do you think that when I first married at 22 I planned it that way! It was furthest from my mind and life plan. But things evolved and much of it out of my control.

The Gloria Story – Mrs. Mink I:

It quickly became apparent that when I married Gloria, I was programmed for a battle from day one as to who could control our home: us or Gloria's mother, Francis. Her dad, a kind but beaten soul, had long since abdicated his male role. His life was occupied with selling candy wholesale 12 hours a day and repeating old, stale stories.

I've never forgotten that first skirmish during our wedding reception at a midtown Manhattan hotel. Gloria, on instructions from her mom, came over and requested that I dance with her mother. I asked why? Answer: "Mother says that's the way it's done." From that point (for years), Mother in Jersey City, NJ, would decide how things should be done, over my vociferous objections. My rebellion led to recriminations, anger, rejection, and continual oneupmanships. After fifteen years, we were basically living separate lives; on the surface it may have appeared idyllic; beneath this artificial veneer there was a calculated disdain and animosity.

As I now see it, for Gloria it was an ideal relationship. She had two handsome children – both high achievers – a beautiful home in suburban Long Island within an elegant community, a car, charge accounts at all major stores, and a checking account. As years went by, I spent as little time as possible at home. I joined a myriad of business, sports and social men's groups, rarely being invited or having guests in our huge home. We led separate lives. I came home at night to eat my hamburger alone. When I asked why a hamburger on a bun (McDonald's style), she would reply, "Aren't you fat enough?"

In truth, I assume there are countless families that operate in this fashion for 30-40 years. But for me it was a loveless and lifeless affair. I was terribly unhappy. I had gained a great deal of weight from frustration and misery.

In fairness, I'm certain Gloria could paint an entirely different scenario. But this was my perception in my book. I clearly recall the final scene. It was New Year's Eve. We went to the socially prescribed shul party – "everyone did it." At midnight, the M.C. called out the last moments of our last year together, 1966. At the stroke of 12, all around us couples kissed and embraced. Jerry and Gloria only glared at each other venomously.

As hurtful as the marriage was, so also were my efforts to separate and divorce. It took me years and tons of money before I finally obtained a NY State divorce. Out of respect for the persons alive and deceased, and concern for our two children, now adults, I'll pass over the gory details. On parting, at the final settlement in court, she yelled out, "You can be sure next time I won't marry a junkman!" This part of our divorce pact she kept resolutely. In fact, she married no one.

P. S. After the divorce, she took a state-sponsored examination and became a parole officer – the perfect position for her. Definition: A parole officer decides who is good or bad, who goes to jail or stays free. I paid alimony for more than 20 years and finally made a lump sum payment in lieu of all future alimony. It was evident her Mr. Right would never appear.

BEA
WIFE #2

It probably was a turn of fate. I'd not like to think of it as Divine Intervention. I had experienced fifteen years in an unhappy, loveless, depressing relationship with Gloria. We had begun a yearly practice of taking the family away for the 10-day Christmas period. I had renewed my interest in improving myself physically, first by joining a golf club, playing tennis and now a new found interest in skiing.

As I mentioned before, in order to keep my sanity, discipline and self-respect, I chose to spend as little time as possible at home, where I was made to feel like the paymaster, not the father figure. For several years we had visited the Concord Hotel in the Catskills which had every conceivable sporting facility. On the ski slope I happened upon a single, divorced friend, Joel. He escorted a lady friend and a Bea Siflinger in tow. Introductions were exchanged, and in the small talk it appeared that Bea resided fifteen minutes walking distance from my business location. She was in a Lefrak City apartment, and I was in Woodside, Queens. Bea was the antithesis of my wife, Gloria. She was very attractive, alert and a street-smart person and survivor. Her history – a single child of a loveless marriage, dominated by her mother's sister, her *aunt*, in whose home they all resided. Her father was a marginal earner but a champion park bench checkers player. He transferred his meager weekly earnings to the aunt, who was the divorced mother of twin daughters. Bea, who was far more attractive than the twins, had to find a way early on to survive in this jungle, best suited for a psychologist's doctoral thesis. Bea was constantly left to fend for herself, and out of desperation (similar to myself), at the age of 19 she married one Julius Siflinger, primarily to escape that home.

Julius Siflinger was an artisan furrier. They quickly had two children, Alan and Sandra, and typically, they purchased a small home on Long Island. Within a few years, again like myself, Bea realized that in her efforts to escape her home she had entered an impossible, senseless marriage. They were incompatible. With the aid of psychological counselling, she separated and divorced, totally lacking support from family and friends and was left stranded, with two small children. Towards his offspring, Julie Siflinger was a *pillar of sand* financially and emotionally.

The follow-up of failed child support and surviving on a small salary as a cosmetic salesperson was typical of a million single-parent households. Added to the heavy burden was the behavior of her two children, left to literally run wild on their own when at school and after, as Bea struggled to support their minimal needs and have a social life as well.

Out of nowhere came her savior, riding in a white Cadillac convertible no less, Jerry Mink, the successful businessman, another emotionally wounded casualty.

I returned home from vacation with the family and resumed my activities. A bit of history enters the stage. 1965 – John Lindsay was elected mayor of New York City and chose to confront the all-powerful labor unions. As a result, the entire public transportation system in NYC went on strike on January 1, 1966. With no way to get to work in Manhattan, and dependent on her weekly salary, Bea the Survivor called her neighbor, yours truly, to drive her to work. In short order, a romance developed between two lonely voyagers desperately seeking a safe harbor.

Within a few months, I recognized that this was a decisive crossroad and not a mere flirtation. Bea was anxious to consummate our relationship and not become a woman in the shadows of my life. I could not find the internal strength – though in truth there had been several previous occasions where I had packed to leave but had "reneged." At this point two events occurred. First, Bea wanted me to meet her children. The contrast between my Lisa and Mitchell, part of the social strata where we resided, and her Alan and Sandy, was oceans apart. Did I wish to abandon my children and take on responsibility for the Siflinger offspring? NO WAY! In addition, they were products of a single-parent fractured family. My Lisa and Mitchell were structured. Lisa was always at the top of the class scholastically. Mitchell was now attending Hebrew Day School. Alan and Sandy were truants and non-achievers. I told Bea we had no future together and broke off the relationship. Just prior, she had encouraged me to see the psychologist who assisted her to leave her husband. On my visit to his office, the doctor inquired what was bothering me?

JM: "I'm terribly unhappy in my marriage to Gloria, but I can't find the strength to leave my home and children."

Dr.: "Why not?"

JM: "What will people say if this successful Jewish husband abandons his family?"

Dr.: "Mr. Mink, I don't think you intend to abandon them; merely divorce their mother, right? Second, I'll tell you *"What They'll Say."* The response will surprise you. 'Did you hear Jerry Mink left Gloria and the home?!' On the second day, they'll say, 'Did you hear Jerry Mink left Gloria and the home?' The second day's response will be, 'I heard that yesterday'."

I left the shrink's office confused. In a few days I rented an apartment in the Forest Hills Inn near my office. I came home one afternoon and removed my clothes and personal items while everyone was out.

I remember it like it was today; it was still mid-winter. I asked my old friend and attorney, Dave Ferdinand, z"l,[1] to come over on a Sunday afternoon to our beautiful home. I told Gloria I no longer wished to live with her and proposed divorce, guaranteeing her a continuance of her lifestyle unchanged, the house, weekly allowance, car, checking account, charge cards. Just allow me to pursue my life as I see fit.

Gloria was surprised that I was taking the offensive. She gave no response. Instead she hired an attorney, who, in turn, placed a private detective on my trail. The next few months were traumatic, as her attorney smelled blood, and papers were continually being filed. Gloria, now in revenge, ran up outrageous charges everywhere. I was forced to discontinue her charge accounts. The war was officially declared.

---

1. z"l – to be remembered with a blessing.

I had set up a comfortable residence and planned to have a new life with my children as a weekend father. As covered in the other chapter, on Gloria, Wife #1, Gloria would have none of this. I was denied visiting privileges, even with court orders. I had also discontinued my relationship with Bea, because of the responsibility of dealing with her children. Several months passed. I began enjoying my new freedom. One evening, on returning to my apartment, I found Bea sitting in the lobby of my residential hotel. She wanted to talk, and over coffee she said we could have a life together. Her children were going to summer camp. She would be free and in the fall she would arrange for her ex, Julius S. (now married), to shelter the kids.

In short order, I bought this bogus package. The two kids did go to camp and we enjoyed a wonderful summer. With no progress at all in my separation, I went down to Mexico and arranged a unilateral divorce, acceptable in many states in the USA. That fall, we drove out to Connecticut and got married in a Reform synagogue. It was a wild time, even by my standards. Bea would have the two children stop by on Sundays. We had rented a beautiful apartment in a luxury building in Whitestone, Queens.

One Sunday, after her children came up, the doorman called. The man who had delivered the children (J. Siflinger) had also dropped off their suitcases. Julie wanted no part of being a father. The next few years were difficult, to put it mildly. Bea continued to work in the cosmetics field. She enrolled Alan in a private military school, to control his conduct. Sandra was a continuous truant. After we had Jackie, the combination of the ongoing problems with her two children, (which is really loshen hora), as contrasted to Lisa being married off to an M.D. in the Plaza Hotel in New York and Mitchell attending John Hopkins University as a pre-med student, was too difficult, in my opinion, for Bea to deal with. She served me with separation papers; we again went through the court system for contested support and visitation rights to Jackie, though in truth, Bea was more forthcoming in allowing me to be with Jackie than Gloria had been. Her divorce action in court against me fell apart when a middle-aged babysitter she regularly employed came forward of her own volition and claimed Bea was a poor specimen of a mother, as she disappeared several times a week and left the infant Jackie in her care. (I knew nothing about this prior to her testimony.) We eventually settled in an out-of-court agreement. Shortly after, I left during the Yom Kippur War. Two years later I made aliyah.

Bea never remarried. After over 23 years she is still attractive and resides in Manhattan. Alan moved to the West Coast. After living on a commune, he took a job and is now also settled down, married and raising a family. Sandra is also married with children. I wish them the best.

FORECLOSE THE HOUSE

It has been thirty plus years since I separated from Gloria, but I feel certain that given her nature and the circumstances we would still be caught up in the divorce battle, except for the following scenario. (Hell hath no fury like a woman scorned.)

Our home in East Hills, LI, had been purchased for cash and remained unencumbered for several years, when I decided to make a major improvement to my scrap metal warehouse in Woodside, Queens. For this I needed immediate cash. I placed a five-year balloon mortgage on my home, paying interest only, totally unaware of the eventual ramifications.

Once I had received the unilateral divorce in Mexico, I considered myself able to be married to Bea (under Connecticut law). This made Gloria more entrenched and unyielding. In despair, my old friend and attorney, Dave Ferdinand, resigned from the case as hopeless and handed me the 10-inch high stack of legal documents which had cost me a ton of money, without results.

I had attempted every avenue to reach a mutually agreed settlement. Gloria wanted neither money nor divorce – just revenge. It left me no recourse except to pursue my life. I had reestablished myself with a wife and a new daughter who was a replica of my firstborn, Lisa. We named her Jaqueline Leah Mink. I had purchased an old servants' quarters next to a mansion that served as the club house for a golf course. Interestingly enough, I bought it from Stan Lee, once Stanley Leiberman, formerly of the Bronx, who was about to become very wealthy and famous via Marvel Comics Enterprise and the cartoon characters Spiderman, Captain Marvel, etc. But at that point he was strapped for cash.

Believe it or not – timing is everything in life. Hence, pursuing the divorce was pointless. Lisa was away at school; Mitchell and I had resurrected our relationship over Gloria's objections, and I was working hard with my partners to build Cousins Metal.

When Dave Ferdinand left my divorce scene, I met up with a young lawyer I knew from my Oceanside, LI, days. He felt certain he could close the matter. I said to go ahead – without retainer or fee agreement. One morning I received a call from the bank holding the mortgage on my former home. I had been paying the interest only on the mortgage for five years.

Banker: "Mr. Mink, the mortgage on your home is due for renewal in several months. If you wish, I'll send you the papers to renew it for another five years."

Just as in the comic strips an electric bulb lit up over my head.

I told him I would not renew it.

Banker: "Then you intend to pay the principal?"

JM: "No."

Banker: "That leaves me no alternative; I'll have to foreclose and sell it at auction to regain our equity."

JM: "That's exactly what I want, but first phone my ex-wife's lawyer. You see, we're in the midst of an ugly divorce conflict." I supplied him with the name and telephone number of Gloria's attorney.

Suddenly, five years of stalemate began to dissolve and I was able to get a New York State divorce and Jewish get[1] in short order. I paid off the mortgage, turned over ownership of the home to Gloria, and began the journey of 20 years of alimony payments. I had grasped a straw and was able to extricate myself from an ugly, endless divorce battle.

Naturally, the young attorney handled the final details, and took full credit for the termination of my marriage and the agreements reached and billed me accordingly.

All the jokes about lawyers contain a great deal of truth.

---

1. get – divorce document.

CHECKING OUT PAPA'S STORY –
A VISIT TO MOTHER RUSSIA

It's unreasonable to assume I was not influenced by my father. He definitely taught me a work ethic; I recall his departing for work at 7:15 every morning. In addition, his penurious nature (except at the card table) affects me till today. However, an often repeated remark at the dinner table, regardless of what Mama prepared or where and what we ate had, haunted me for years: "This can't compare to a piece of herring, real black bread and white potatoes that we ate in Glubuka" (his shtetl in Lithuania).

Historical Background

The combination of Stalin and Hitler (Satan's messengers) imposed a dreadful toll on all mankind. We Jews being of lesser number, suffered the most, losing one third of our total population. The barbarities of Joseph Stalin are still being unearthed over 40 years after his death in 1953.

At this point, the two major powers, the USA and the USSR, were locked in a titanic struggle for the survival of their respective ideologies. Fortunately, the two were evenly balanced in conventional and nuclear weaponry of total destruction. There had even been periodic flare-ups: Korea, Hungary, Cuba, Vietnam. Fortunately, the antagonists kept their own armaments holstered. In the late 1950's, with the ascendancy of Nikita Khrushchev as dictator of Russia, unexpectedly there appeared a minute fissure in the wall of belligerence. Surprisingly, an advertisement appeared in the New York Times inviting foreigners to join organized tours and visit the USSR.

Acting on impulse as usual, I responded and received a rather prompt response: "Please explain why you wish to visit the USSR. What are your interests, which areas do you wish to visit." I listed Moscow, the Black Sea resort of Sochi (where Khrushchev had his summer home) and the scrap industry in Russia. Again, in a surprisingly brief period, my letter and requests were acknowledged. I was told that this combination would not be part of any organized tour, but rather a private visit. I agreed. All costs were paid in advance (very expensive). The exchange rate then was $1.50=1 ruble. (Today it is $1.00 = appr. 5,000 rubles!). Nervously, Gloria and I went off to Russia for two weeks. The only air transport was via KLM. (USA planes were not welcome.) The trip, pre-jet plane era, was endless. New York-Newfoundland-Ireland-Amsterdam-finally, Moscow. On arrival, prior to our leaving the plane, a team of KGB police interrogated us. In that one moment I felt certain the next stop was the Gulag in Siberia. Prior to leaving the States, I made inquiries as to what to expect in Russia of the 1950's. Eventually, I was *mis*directed to a Professor Block at Queens College, NYC, the "Russian Jewish Expert." The professor congratulated me on my resolve and suggested how we could assist our fellow Jews in the USSR. The list of essentials needed were: prayer books, tfillin, and, most important, YIDDISH newspapers. I visited lower Manhattan, stocked up on the religious items and visited the Yiddish newspaper The Forward, purchasing 30 copies of dated editions.

Disappointment #1

We were received at the Moscow airport by a guide, Ivan, and private car, and driven to the first class hotel across from the Kremlin – The National. The guide was a language student and a candidate for Russia's foreign service. He was particularly interested in our langue usage and idioms, and life in the States. He carried on a continuous propaganda dialogue during the drive to the hotel and the following several days.

We unpacked, noted the primitive bathroom and other modest facilities. *Now*, the time had finally arrived to check out Papa's delicacy. Entering the dining room, we were handed a menu in at least six languages. A polite, English-speaking head waiter approached. "What would our American guests like? May I suggest...?" I brought him up short. "I know exactly what I wish to order." I scanned the menu. Yes, there it was – herring. "Herring, black bread, and potatoes." Finally, the real thing!

The surprised head waiter tried to dissuade me. "Sir, are you sure? These are really *peasant foods!*" I assured him I knew exactly what I was ordering. What a disappointment. They were the same foods as in the States, except the bread was much heavier and more filling. Pop, you misled me again. But these were his childhood fantasies.

Disappointment #2

That afternoon we arrived at the famous GUM Department Store of several floors. Huge, but totally lacking variety. If you wanted a hat, it was brown only. Shoes, crude and black. Everything thereafter functional – that's it. Walking in the streets, everyone seemed to be looking down. When they saw our shoes, they looked up – foreigners. The next morning, our guide, Ivan, and car arrived at 8 a.m. "Where would you like to go, sir?" "To the main synagogue." When we packed our clothes in the States, we had lined the cases with the newspapers, etc. Shlepping it all in a large sack, we arrived at the synagogue to meet Rabbi Levin, then Chief Rabbi. We were able to converse in Yiddish. When I disclosed I had smuggled in the 30 copies of the Yiddish newspaper, he whispered in alarm, "Our conversation may be recorded. I beg you, take them back to your hotel and destroy them at once. This is a serious criminal offense." After distributing some tzedaka (charity) and the religious items, I returned to the hotel and spent the balance of that first day tearing the 30 newspapers into small pieces and depositing them down the antiquated toilet facilities, very cautiously.

Disappointment #3

When I requested the guide to show us their scrap metal operations, he remarked: "We do not invite foreigners to our Mother Country to exhibit garbage dumps (his English)." We drove about Moscow for several days, always under the direction of our tour guide. We saw the magnificent ballet, toured the spotless, orderly subway system, whose depth, hundreds of feet below street level via express escalators, appeared to be shelters against atomic bomb attack.

A note in passing: On the original trip from airport to hotel, we crossed a minor bridge of perhaps 100 meters. The guide announced proudly, "This bridge was constructed by the workers of the USSR in 145 days." Trying to be a pleasant guest, I answered, "Remarkable." Unfortunately, thereafter, each time we crossed we heard the same gloating sales pitch – 145 days – at least six times. Finally, on the final drive back to the airport, as we crossed the aformentioned bridge again, I asked Ivan to stop. I left to inspect the bridge carefully (Mink, the bridge expert). "Ivan, you have never been to the States or outside Russia. Please hear me carefully. If the United States *really* wanted to complete this bridge in record time, we could do it in 60 days."

The final stop was Sochi on the Black Sea. It was unimpressive, except for the size of their cockroaches.

We returned to the States convinced this contest of national will and capabilities was a mismatch.

YECHEZKEL AND RABBI MOSHE FEINSTEIN

I was on a non-stop business trip flight from Los Angeles to New York in a first-class cabin (at my company's expense). I became engaged in an intimate conversation with a very charming receptionist-type – not an airline hostess – who assists first-class passengers.

It was definitely leading toward an evening involvement, but I couldn't make it. I had arranged to receive my "get" (Jewish divorce) that evening at a Bet Din in lower Manhattan.

The arrangements were facilitated by Rabbi Seymour Baumrind, z"l, of the Lake Success Jewish Center. I had resided there as a single man again, after the civil divorce from Wife II, Beatrice a.k.a. Bayla. We met at the pre-arranged location, and Rabbi Baumrind explained he had arranged for a Bet Din organized by Rabbi Tendler (Rav Moshe Tendler's father), who had gathered the necessary quorum.

When we arrived at the senior Tendler's apartment, the rabbi asked forgiveness. He could not officiate; his wife was ill. However, he had asked his son's machatonim (in-laws) to deal with the matter. When Rabbi Baumrind realized that Rav Moshe Feinstein would officiate, he was overwhelmed and cried, "Jerry, we are going to be invited to the home of the Posek HaDor (religious authority of this generation)!" I was way out of my league, having zero awareness of religious hierarchy. We walked a few hundred yards from one apartment block to the next and were presently in the home of Rav Moshe Feinstein, z"l.

After being greeted, Rav Moshe began questioning me about my history; a divorce document had to be written, and only in the proper way. What surprised me was that Rav Moshe was constantly being called away to the phone. I was ignorant of the fact that religious figures from all corners of the world were continually presenting him with religious shielas (questions).

Just about the time we were concluding our procedure, an incredible and unforgettable event occurred. The front door bell rang and Rebbetzin Feinstein answered. There was a brief exchange between her and a mother and teenage son. On entering, the mother and son remained standing just inside the door and observed Rav Moshe. Curious, I asked the Rebbetzin what was going on. She replied that this young man and his mother had come from Toronto, and he had requested, as a bar mitzvah present, to have an opportunity just to *look at* Rav Moshe. The Toronto mother and son stood for ten minutes transfixed, looking at Rav Moshe, and left. Recalling this occurrence, I realized the enormity of the events that entered my life by Divine Intervention.

MY MAMA

It was obvious that this was to be the most difficult chapter of my auto-biography to record.

I have long realized that I experienced my ultimate pain and loss prior to my 20th year. Previously I recorded I had left NYU before graduation. It's now obvious why: There was no one to bring my report card home to.

It has been many years since I dedicated a library and garden in my mother's memory. That is for public expression, but in my heart there has been a grieving spot for the past 50 years.

My earliest and fondest memories are of my loving and caring Mama. With, at best, an 8th grade level evening school education, she made sure to read the New York Post daily, with columnists Max Lerner, Eleanor Roosevelt, and Dorothy Thompson her favorites. I can hear it now; I'd walk into the house from high school or college and she would be waiting with, "Jerry, you must hear this," and she would read a section of one of these columnists. I alone shared her intellectual strength and insight.

Background

In several chapters, I gave snippets of Mama's history: her parents Nochum Haim and Shoshana Gering. She was one of seven surviving children. Two boys, Avraham and Elyakim, died as youngsters. This astounding story has just surfaced as I prepared this biography.

Mama would tell me often about walking out – *yes, walking out of Poland* – north to Danzig, now called Gdansk. I never really comprehended this information as a youngster, or even as a teenager (who was wrapped up in his own adventures). One of the memorabilia I have retained as I entered many ports was my mother's original exit visa from Poland, #708, dated November 6, 1920, issued to a Leia Gering. The next entry is her arrival (with her sister Dorothy) on December 15, 1920, in Danzig. The final recording is January 19, 1921, leaving for the USA. The story she had told me when I was a boy was her walk out of Poland. Following WWI and the revolution in Russia (Poland being a territory of Russia at the time), the Polish army was fighting the Germans, then the Russians. The German army, under Kaiser Wilhelm, entering and retreating. The Russian army of the Tzar fighting the Poles and then the Germans. The White Russians fighting the Red Russians, the Communists, etc., etc. Armies came in, sacked the country time and time again over six years.

My mama, Chaya Leah Gering, leaving Bialystok for America, 1921

Mama with daughter Selma and son Jerry (the author)

By 1920 the economy and the transportation system were in shambles. So with a small sum, my stouthearted mother, aged 20, and her next older sister, Dorothy, aged 18, began the trek north during the winter of 1920.

The trip took over a month (verified by the visa dates). The distance (I checked in a world atlas) was 400 kilometers, or about 270 miles. Carrying 2 satchels, avoiding marauding soldiers and highwaymen, taught by tradition to eat only kosher foods, they finally got to Danzig, hoping to find a Jewish home to accept them. But the German Jews were disdainful of these refugees, and they stayed in a hovel for a month.

Hence I can understand the fortitude and inner strength now shown by my two daughters who strongly resemble their grandmother in appearance and fortitude. Both are named after her, Leah and Chaya Leah.

On arrival in the States, the sisters went to live with Aunt Gussy. (See chapter, Aunt Dotty and the 30's...) Both Mama and Dorothy found jobs in the garment industry. In the building where Aunt Gussy Segal resided were neighbors Louis and Sonia Friedman, my father's sister and brother-in-law. The shidduch was made between my mother and father, and the product of that union, Yechezkel, is now writing this autobiography. As I indicated before, it was a terrible mismatch of an enlightened, cultured, beautiful woman and a brute from the Pale in Lithuania. My father was totally illiterate; he could barely sign his name and made up for his inadequacy by abusing Mama, and at times me, when a boy. But he was a modest, though tight-fisted, provider. At some point in 1942 Mama began to complain about pains in her chest. It was discovered she had breast cancer. A massive mastectomy was performed at Memorial Hospital in Manhattan. Chemotherapy and other sophisticated techniques were 20 or more years distant. For 4½ years Mama suffered silently in pain. I remember during the war she would utter, "If only Hitler had these pains he would leave the Jews alone." As I mentioned to earlier, her parents had passed on before the Germans could lay a hand on them. But her two sisters, Rifka and Faigie, and their families, were turned into ashes in Hitler's furnaces. Mama cried bitter tears for months on end.

In May 1947, she had a recurrence of the cancer. It had spread to her nervous system. She went into a coma and remained in a number of local and Manhattan hospitals and nursing homes, to no avail. On July 13, 1947, Mama left this world and my life forever, leaving behind two grieving children. Over the years I have never heard anyone say a negative word about this tzaddekes. She was always willing to be a friend to the most downtrodden, whether a relative or stranger. Now, 50 years later, my heart cries over my loss. Without any reservation, whatever goodness and chesed I possess, I inherited from my Mama.

UNCLE GEORGE AND SONS

After Mama's passing, I concluded my formal education at NYU after three years and out of despair worked for several months in Papa's scrap yard. One of the people with whom we did business was a scrap dealer in Lynbrook, Louie Friedman. Louie was a typical oddball scrap dealer – who had taken over the business of one Tom Pellegrino, who was childless (no one to turn over the business to), and quite wealthy (for the times). He had operated his scrap business for 30 plus years and decided to retire. Tom could best be described as the Godfather-type, impeccably attired, carrying an Old World air of respectability, with a perennial stogie in the corner of his mouth.

Louie Friedman ran the scrap yard a few years but wanted out badly. My Uncle George was complaining bitterly about being frozen in for five months a year at Albany, NY. (He also had purchased an established scrap business from the Kudon Family, whose sons were not interested in the junk business.) On my own initiative, putting 2 and 2 together, I called Uncle George from a pay phone in the corner drugstore. No one would dare make a long distance call – perhaps $0.50 – from the recently acquired house phone.

Uncle George came down the next weekend and together the 20 year old nephew, Jerry Mink, and 45 year old Uncle George began negotiating to buy the business. When it came to tachlis,[1] George did not have sufficient capital to close the deal. So, I went to Papa, told him the story and borrowed $10,000. I now recognize that the $10,000 loan was conscience money, because on the

---

1. tachlis – practical matters.

Mink. the Scrapman, 1960, the "working days," a caricature

night Mama left us, I verbally assaulted Papa with all my recollections of the horrendous life he had given Mama and his children. All 19 years of pent-up rage and anger were unleashed, and he cowered under the verbal attack. So the loan, which was not really in his nature, was given as a form of recognition of guilt, compensation and restitution.

After signing notes to Papa, I became a partner. George invested about $16,000. The partnership was irrational and untenable. In less than a year, George bought me out and I returned the $10,000 to Papa. The truth is, it did *not* proceed as smoothly as I relate. Uncle George passed on many years ago. During his lifetime I idealized him as Mama's brother and for his independence. (Remember the decision not to change his name.) Also, he was always very liberal in his politics. I guess he was one of my role models.

I came out with $1,500 profit after drawing a minimal $25/week salary. The remainder must remain unsaid as it would be loshen hora, for I was really tossed out. With that $1,500, I bought my first used truck to go peddling as described previously. (See chapter: My Uncle George: The Early Years.) Uncle George's business prospered. He eventually bought the Pellegrino property – we had been tenants originally – also, additional land next door and a very nice home in East Rockaway. When his boys, Shelly and Norman, became adults, they married and joined him in the business.

All this from the $0.50 telephone call to Albany that I made years before. But, as I recall, similar to many things I've done, it was never acknowledged.

WHATEVER HAPPENED TO HARRIET?

On many occasions, events have occurred to me that I felt were worth telling; as a consequence, this autobiography.

For perhaps 25-30 years my professional accountant, both in business and personal affairs, was Martin Rosen of Martin Rosen and Co., NYC. Marty was and is a good friend and a proud Jew. But that's not our story.

As my business activities decreased, Marty's grew significantly. At some point, after my aliyah, I was assigned to one of his associates, Michael Lipsky. We arrived at a yearly routine whereby, a month or so prior to tax time, I would notify Michael of a date and time I would visit his office with all my year-end papers. It proved mutually satisfactory. Routinely, we would exchange small talk about our lives. Michael would tell his secretary to hold all calls for half an hour.

Some ten years ago this unbelievable event occurred. It was the annual visit; his secretary was instructed to hold all calls. Just as we got into particulars, suddenly his phone rang.

Michael, annoyed: "Why are you disturbing us?"

Secretary explains: "A senior IRS agent is calling, demanding information on an audit, *immediately.*"

This was a top priority situation. Michael apologized and took the call.

Michael: "Mr. Heilbronner, I want you to know you're interrupting a meeting set a month ago, and Mr. Jerry Mink, a client, has just flown in from Jerusalem, Israel." (An attempt to show deference to the senior agent and at the same time let him know he was disturbing us.)

The agent replied (shocking Michael): "Ask Mr. Jerry Mink if he went to Public School 73 in East New York, Brooklyn, and if he remembers his school friend in third grade – some fifty years ago – Charles Heilbronner?"

At that point, Michael hands me the phone. We were both astounded and Charles H. invited me to his home for a visit.

As in many such cases, the minor common events of fifty years ago had dissolved into trivia. Charles was unrecognizable and in an entirely different life stream than the Israeli Yechezkel Mink. Until I asked the question, "Whatever happened to Harriet?" obviously not the woman he married. But a lifetime ago we had both fiercely vied for her attention. In the interim, the three adults had taken other directions.

ALPHONSE, MARIO AND JERRY MINK

Nassau County, with a population in the 1960's of 1,500,000, was divided into a number of townships. Hempstead Township, with perhaps ten smaller villages or subdivisions, was the most populous. Basically, it was a bedroom community of ex-NYC escapees and commuters. Oceanside was one such village. At that point we purchased the property in Oceanside for our business. Shelly, my partner, insisted we use his attorney, a certain Billy Finger – since disbarred and deceased at a young age. (A book could also be written about his exploits.) Since we planned to employ my friend Marty Rosen as our accountant, it seemed fair: my accountant, his lawyer. When we started operating, it was on an industrial site with a small stream at the back of the bulkheaded (wooden supported) property. Remember its name – Oceanside. Suitable only for small pleasure crafts, after about five years, several small homes were built by a developer on the opposite side of the stream.

In a minor oversight, Mr. Finger failed to investigate the Hempstead Town Hall Registry for any exceptions to the properties' usages. This was the onset of another very painful conflict. It seemed that one of the new homeowners did not appreciate having a scrap yard practically in his backyard (just on the other side of the stream). He visited the Registry Office and there it was, clearly stated for any layman to see: "This property cannot be used as an auto wrecking facility."

Factually, we were not in that business, but the Hempstead supervisor, a minor local politician, was none other than Alphonse D'Amato. (Yes, now the New York State senator.) Having aspirations to move on politically, Mr.

D'Amato decided here was something to "hang his hat on," improper usage of industrial land – "an environmental disgrace."

Unbeknown to us, one bright day a representative of Hempstead Township handed us a summons to appear in court based on this technicality. As the president of the firm, I appeared. The local District Court Judge looked over the summons and heard the statement of the lawyer for the town. In a clearly politically motivated move – I'm certain engineered by Alphonse for its sensational value – we were summarily ordered to close up shop and leave the facility in three months, over my shocked objections. I had gone to court without an attorney, considering it merely a nuisance complaint, similar to a traffic ticket. The aforementioned attorney, Mr. Finger, was no longer practicing law after being disbarred, but operating a very successful dance club on L.I. We desperately needed major legal surgery, not first aid.

The next day, it was a major story breaking in Newsday, the L.I. paper. I was interviewed and claimed foul play and that Alphonse was employing it for its full news value. The tale expands. At that point in time, one of our scrap clients was Horn Construction, whose principals I knew from my board membership in H.A.N.C. (Hebrew Academy of Nassau County). Moe Hornstein, president of Horn, was the major benefactor of that institution, and his son-in-law, Gene Goldman, and I became friendly, initially via the day school and later through business. Horn Construction was a major highway and infrastructure contractor in the Metropolitan area. In desperation, I phoned Gene for advice. He recommended that we retain the services of an old line Brooklyn Court Street legal firm with several Irish names, one being a former NYS Supreme Court judge. Gene also suggested that we specifically ask for one of the junior partners, a very talented attorney and spokesman, Mario Cuomo.

In a phone conversation, I introduced myself to Mario, using Gene Goldman's name profusely, as though I was family. I explained our problem – saying I thought "this is something right up your alley" – and arranged an appointment. In a few days, accompanied by my partner Shelley, we met Mario at his offices. He was a real charmer and clearly a legal talent. We gave him the details of our crisis. After hearing us out, Mario replied, "I'll take the case. Our initial retainer will be $10,000." This was really the Major Leagues!!

Shelly and I were in shock. In 1970 this was a bloody fortune. Mario, seeing our chagrin, said, "I'll leave you boys alone for 10 minutes to decide." We had no choice. Our livelihood and what we had developed, plus our investment, were on the line.

The next scene should have been recorded for a major film!!

After requesting an appeal on the District Judge's verdict of evacuation in three months, we reappeared a few weeks later, now with our attorney of record, Mario and his associate, plus a pile of legal tomes. On the bench was the same District Court judge (who usually dealt with minor municipal offenses for the Township of Hempstead). A political appointee lawyer represented the Township. (His usual activities were probably as a political organizer during election periods for the local Republican machine.) Mario arose. "Your Honor, I now represent the firm Cousins Metal Industries to argue in opposition to your earlier decision on the Township's complaint. We have presented papers to the court to support our contention. In the case of X vs. New Hampshire, the State Supreme Court ruled....etc., etc., etc." The political hack Town Attorney was grasping for straws in this now deep legal morass. As Mario continued, the judge also realized this was not a sand lot game, but the Major Leagues. It was music to our ears to hear the talented attorney Cuomo defend us.

Judge: "I'd like to speak to the learned counselors in my chambers."

Bottom Line: The decision for closure was rescinded until the two parties, Cousins and the Township, could work out a mutually acceptable resolution, which we accomplished.

Mario was now our hero and became my personal friend. He and his wife, Matilda, were invited and attended to my daughter Lisa's wedding. About twenty years later when, as Governor of New York State, he visited Israel, we partook in a memorable Friday night dinner together in the company of his entourage, including a New York rabbi and many Israeli functionaries. What a guy!

A SECOND FORAY INTO POLITICS

Mario Cuomo

When it was announced that Mario would be the candidate for Lieutenant Governor in New York State, alongside Hugh Carey, I called up and inquired how my company could help. Mario was our hero, and had saved our backsides a short time before. (Chapter: Alphonse, Mario and J. Mink) Within a few days, a representative came around and we made a sizable contribution – mostly in recognition for his legal help to save our business. I also really believed in his good, honest, political commitment.

A few months passed and the election campaign was heating up. One of his aides came by to see me at the office. Could I help sponsor a rally in my area of Southwest Nassau County? A brilliant idea crossed my mind; how about a brunch on my lawn? My home (I was divorced again) stood on 1½ acres in a residential district, across from a golf course. Great setting for an outdoor event. The campaign committee gave enthusiastic approval.

It would be a bagel and lox extravaganza.

I began organizing. First, I got my son, Mitchell, to bring a number of his school friends (whom I would pay) to be car attendants. I retained a staff to act as waiters. I bought hundreds of bagels, a huge mound of cream cheese, hundreds of dollars worth of lox, coffee, soda, milk, etc. I had placed signs in all directions leading to my home and ads in local papers. We awaited the onslaught. At 12 sharp, Mario arrived with his entourage to welcome the guests and deliver a short speech. It was a brilliant day, with everything in place beforehand. Unbelievably, perhaps only 25 people showed up. There was more staff than guests. In depression, we tried to laugh it off. But it wasn't funny; all that food; all that money; all that work.

Well, Mario and Carey were elected in spite of my failed effort. The clock now moves forward some 20 years. Governor Cuomo is now in his second term as New York State Governor and in 1993 decided to visit Israel. We made contact on his arrival. My wife, BatSheva, and I were invited to an unforgettable Friday night private dinner at the King David Hotel. As we entered the private room, Mario introduced me to his entourage as "a dear friend from Long Island, NY." At this point, one of his aides came over and opened, "Are you *the* Jerry Mink? You may not know, but you're a legend."

During Mario's second gubernatorial campaign, a giant dinner rally was staged at the Garden City Hotel main ballroom. After thanking the crowd of perhaps 1,500 for attending this fundraiser on Long Island, the Governor continued his remarks with, "Where were you when my friend, Jerry Mink, made his bagel and lox brunch?" He then detailed that campaign non-starter, etc, to much applause and laughter.

In the recent Netanyahu vs. Peres competition I was out once more on the streets, doing my thing for Bibi, and it proved more successful.

THE NY FOOTBALL GIANTS
VS
DR. SOL ROGATNICK

It definitely was shaping up as the game of the year, for the leadership of the Eastern Division of the National Football League. For days the NY Post had been devoting eight pages in its sports section to statistics – commentary and match ups. The NY Giants vs the Washington Redskins. Y.A. Tittle vs Sonny Jerguson, the Giant defense of Andy Robustelli, Rosy Grier, Sam Huff and Co. Could they stop the ferocious Redskins, overwhelm the opposing Quarterback, obviously crucial matters. Having been for years a purchaser of upscale tickets with my cousins, the Gerings, plus my friends, the DeMatteos and Attonitos, these games were the object of endless discourse, almost lehavdil[1] a religion, and a case of NY pride. They were played vicariously by a million Giant fans each Sunday. This week, Yechezkel again was all set for the AWAY game. The TV was well positioned in the den, the goodies placed in strategic locations within arms reach.

1:05 p.m. – kickoff! The ball was arching high and long toward the enemy Redskins; suddenly the front door bell rings. Who could be calling now? The Rogatnicks, Dr. Sol and Corrine. I ran to open the door and yelled at Sol, "Your timing is great, the game has just begun."

Sol: "What game?"

---

1. lehavdil – not to be even remotely compared to.

Now allow me to pause and introduce Dr. Sol Rogatnick (since deceased at an early age), my friend for many years. Sol had been my former wife's obstetrician when my daughter Jackie (now the light of my life) had been conceived. Early on, it had been determined that this was a case of inverted placenta (the baby was lying in a reverse position for exit). Dr. Sol, as a friend and professional, dealt with this case in what must be called a hands-on fashion, and managed to reverse the position of the child, so that where we had expected a Caesarian section, we had a normal birth, and a gorgeous girl, Jacqueline Leah Mink.

Back to the scenario. Impossible! Dr. Sol, a red blooded American, not interested in the Big Game? I sat dutifully in the living room but kept dodging into the den every few minutes to catch the TV action. Finally, the Rogatnicks arose, clearly perturbed. Sol exclaimed, "I came to visit the Minks, but they are obviously busy." And left in a huff. In the annals of football statistics who knows who won that Sunday game. First thing Monday morning I was on the phone, relating the incident to my sports-minded associates. Needless to say, it was a kangaroo court. All agreed that the Rogatnicks were out of line; imagine visiting unannounced on Sunday, at game time no less!!

The time clock moves forward some ten years, and Yechezkel is seated in the Bais Medrash (study room) of the Diaspora Yeshiva reviewing with his class the parasha (weekly portion) in Genesis, which relates how Avraham, our Father, was sitting in his tent three days after he had circumcised himself. He was in intense pain, plus it was a scorching hot day. And he was conversing with no less an entity than Hashem. In the distance he perceived three strangers approaching his tent. Avraham leapt to his feet, directed Sarah, his wife, to shecht (slaughter) a goat and prepare a feast, as he ran out to greet his guests and wash their feet after the journey.

Avraham, was being put to the TEST by Hashem and passed with flying colors. Suddenly, as I recalled how I dealt with the Rogatnicks, my unannounced guests, my new evaluation was traumatizing. On my next visit to the States, I called Dr. Sol and explained I had something to discuss. I called at his home, explained that I was now a ba'al teshuva[1] learning Torah and

---

1. ba'al teshuva – returnee to religious observance.

acquiring new insights on life, and had come to realize the great injustice I had perpetrated on him years ago. I asked him to grant me mechila.[1] Sol looked at me as though I had just landed from Mars, could not relate to any of it. I left with the matter unresolved.

Unfortunately, it was the last time I was to see Dr. Sol. However, it became for me a lesson in the reality of the Living Torah.[2]

---

1. mechila – a pardon; forgiveness.
2. Living Torah – pertinent for all generations, now and forever.

DR. MARVIN WERTHEIM'S PRESCRIPTION

From childhood, I was always described as a chubby. In fact, I remember Mama could only find clothes for me in Boxer's Store Basement (on Pitkin Avenue, in Brooklyn). We would never bother to look for anything on the main floor selection for regular boys.

The only time I trimmed down was in the Navy and a few years after.

But the frustration of my unsuccessful marriage led to eating orgies and the pounds multiplied. I had made it a practice to take a yearly physical, perhaps the in thing at that time in my life. Each year, Dr. Marvin Wertheim, our G.P. (now called internist), would give me the various tests and his comments: "Pressure good, cholesterol OK, but Jerry, I have a chart of your weight; it only goes up."

Employing great psychological insight, Dr. W completed another year's exam with a new shtick.[1] He handed me the bill and an envelope – with the inscription *Only open as prescribed*.

JM: "What's this, Doc?"

Dr. W: "Jerry, I'm predicting in the next few years, based on your weight escalation, you will have a serious heart attack. IF YOU SURVIVE IT, open the envelope to see how close I came to the date!"

Within a year, I became active in sports (as described in another chapter) and lost 40 ugly pounds.

It's an ongoing battle, but I weigh in every morning and battle my love of goodies, especially cake and ice cream, in daily skirmishes.

---

1. schtick – manner of dealing with.

COUSINS METAL INDUSTRIES

The final seven years of my business career in America, as the president of Cousins Metal Industries, were my most profitable and also established my cousins, the brothers Shelly and Norman Gering, to be financially secure. As noted previously, as a 20 year old, I had gone into business in 1948 with my Uncle George Gering. How this occurred was detailed in Uncle George and Sons. After we separated, I described how I went back to peddling on a truck, etc.

Eventually, after Papa's passing, I took over his business in Corona, Queens, and began to expand it significantly. In a few years, his facility was much too small. I sold that property and moved to a larger location in Woodside, Queens. Over several years, I expanded the business further and bought properties on both sides of my operation, and continued to expand. With the separation and painful divorce from Gloria, and my being distanced from my children, I lost my drive and enthusiasm. For whom was I building a business? My children were not any part of my life, my son Mitchell was never going to be a junkman under any circumstances; he was just too much of a straight arrow.

But timing is everything. One afternoon, a real estate agent stopped by to inquire if I wanted to sell or rent my property. It set my mind into motion. Why not? Between rent income and possibly working for another scrap operation, life would be less stressful. (In the late 1960's, there were many mergers, and a number of scrap dealers and smelters had been bought up by public companies.) So on impulse, I placed an ad, without mentioning my name, in the trade paper and was pleased to receive many responses. I began negotiating to rent my warehouse to a wholesale lumber and building supply operation. I would have: a. my rent income, b. a job with significantly less personal pressure, and c. my working capital invested in an income-producing equity. Between the three, more than enough to live comfortably. This was all before I was 40.

But it did not work out that way. Divine Intervention?

This is just when my Uncle George had taken his two married sons into the Merrick Scrap Metal Co. (my original company). Over a period of 15-20 years, the wounds from our original business involvement had healed, and I saw that Shelly was a very competent and aggressive businessman – always looking for new areas in which to expand.

They also had a problem of another nature. The original Pellegrino Property which Uncle George had purchased was now located on an important thoroughfare, and after 20 years was a very valuable equity. The local municipality did not fancy having a scrap yard at the town entrance and harassed the Gerings continually. Under pressure, they purchased land in Oceanside, LI. The work, time and money it would take to utilize and convert this property, totally lacking in any infrastructure, would be enormous.

The Gerings and I spoke often, since we also did some trading. I discussed our divergent paths. One day, I inquired about a property on a large tract of land a mile away from them. It appeared boarded up and abandoned. Shelly said the price was out of sight. I asked for the telephone number to call, which was located on a billboard behind a fenced-off area. Meanwhile, the Gerings were negotiating with a local Cadillac agency to sell their scrap yard property to them.

I called the billboard number and was transferred to the boss's son – just the job for a boss's son, answering nudnick calls. Background: the property was owned by a public company manufacturing ladies underwear. The building had been an adjunct to a merger made several years earlier. In its present condition, it was not fit for manufacturing, but was perfect for a scrap warehouse. Junior ran to Dad, president of corporation, and probably said, "I have a live one to take this headache and yearly real estate tax burden off our hands."

After making an appointment for the next day, I called Shelly. We arrived and were ushered into the offices of this ex-Brooklyn Jewish, obviously former roughneck, now president of a stock exchange listed company. He greeted us in his bedroom slippers, and the following dialogue ensued.

Ex-Brooklynite: "You two kids got money or are you just bulls_____?"

At that point I was 40 and Shelly 28.

The kids: "Yes, we are serious and yes, we have cash money."

Ex-Brooklynite (who used an expletive every third or fifth word – mostly the "F" word in various derivatives – continued the conversation), "I can't lower the price, but we'll take back a major portion in the form of a mortgage at a low interest rate."

In short order we shook hands on a deal. So now, twenty years later, the Gerings and I were partners again. Pouring most of our capital into revamping the property and new equipment, we were constantly short of money and pressed. But, fortunately, in time, we found a vice-president at Chemical Bank, Jerry Nardiello, who had confidence in us and gave us a credit line to get on our feet, and eventually prosper.

When I proposed leaving for the Yom Kippur War, they might have been more solicitous, and when I chose to make aliyah, they were very difficult, but this was my life decision, and I had to "pay" for it. There were also difficult negotiations in dividing the real estate we owned jointly. Shelly eventually told mutual friends it was the best deal he had made up to that point, buying me out. Whatever the chemistry was, we complemented each other's abilities. My cousins, the Gerings, are today wealthy businessmen, and I have had my Zionist bent and my Zadah's wish fulfilled.

THOUGHTS ON RETIRING
TO FLORIDA

By the 1970's our scrap business was extremely profitable. The Gering Brothers' parents (my Uncle George and Aunt Edith) had sold their Long Island home and purchased a condominium apartment in the Miami, Florida, suburbs. The brothers were traveling south frequently to visit and vacation.

At a regular company meeting, they proposed the firm should purchase a condominium for our convenience – why not! In short order, as we did everything else – Shelly and I flew down one morning to a prearranged meeting at a vacation colony named Fountains of West Palm Beach, Florida. That evening we returned as owners of a vacation abode.

A few months later, we flew down and, in one day, chose a decorator, selected wallpaper, color schemes, furniture, appliances, kitchenware, etc., and assigned a strict budget. This was typical of Shelly and myself. *We just did it*. This was our common denominator and probably the source of our business success as well.

Within a few months the condominium was available for occupancy. It was a truly lovely setting, sited on a golf course within the confines of an upscale country club environment. It was fully furnished and always prepared for vacationing. When at last I took advantage of the facility I spent an entire week, playing tennis, resting, going out each evening for dinner. Every day was a replay of the previous.

The final decider for me was the additional ritual of daily mall or supermarket shopping. The spectacle of hundreds of *harnessed* former business people and professionals and their mates winding through the aisles and making the major daily decision of whether to purchase, e.g., the family-size corn flakes or the single-serving packs. For countless hordes this was their Gan Eden (Paradise). For Jerry Mink, I saw it as a case of terminal mental paralysis and a return to the final great elephant burial ground.

Given all its problems and madness – see the chapters Only in Israel – I chose Israel, where you can die of many things but never of boredom.

CHRONOLOGY OF YOM KIPPUR WAR EVENTS – MY DECISION TO MAKE ALIYAH

October 6, 1973: Syria and Egypt launch Yom Kippur War.

October 12: Yechezkel departs for Israel.

October 18: Climactic meeting with Shoshana Weidenfeld at kibbutz kitchen. My basic decision to eventually make aliyah.

October 22: Cessation of hostilities on both fronts.

April 2, 1974: Agranat Commission recommends that Chief of Staff David Elazar be relieved of command.

April 11, 1974: Prime Minister Golda Meir hands in her resignation. She had assumed her share of responsibility for Yom Kippur losses.

The year 1976 found Golda Meir, former Israeli prime minister, on a lecture tour across the USA, defending the Jewish State. This is after the United Nations, on November 10, 1975, overwhelmingly adopted the vicious anti-Israel resolution identifying Zionism as racism.

The Jew was once again standing alone before the world's assembly.

One morning, I scanned the New York Times, which I had delivered to me daily. Golda was at a Midwestern University (I think Indiana), on her cross-country journey. Following her set address, she was responding to audience participation queries. This one caught my attention.

"Who should make aliyah, Golda?" Her response was critical to me; it was there in print:

"No one can dictate who shall come and live in Israel. It is a paramount, yet personal decision for *each* Jew." The question was now who will decide for you,

Jerry Mink! I pondered it over several hundred times. It eventually jump-started my aliyah engine into motion.

To quote Rabbi Shlomo Riskin:

"There are no Orthodox rabbis outside of Israel; they have all decided to Reform the Torah commandment, *Lech Lecha*.[1]

Perhaps they have all forgotten that the Torah is not a novel but rather an instruction book sent by Hashem through his messenger Moshe Rabbeinu.

In 1988, on the 40th anniversary of the rebirth of the State of Israel, I assembled a 20-page booklet in conjunction with my teacher, Rabbi Jeremy

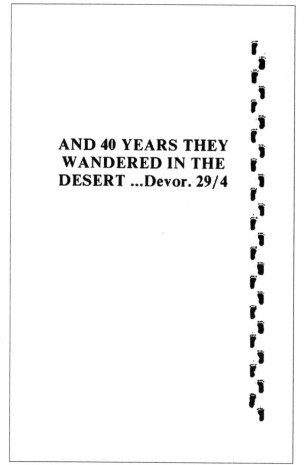

AND 40 YEARS THEY WANDERED IN THE DESERT ...Devor. 29/4

"And 40 Years They Wandered"; booklet by the author and his rabbi; distributed to hundreds of synagogues

---

1. Commandment to our father Abraham to travel to Israel.

Fenster. It was a composite of numerous directives from Torah, Talmud, Seforim and Midrashic sources concerning aliyah. I had it printed and mailed to several hundred Orthodox synagogues and institutions in North America. (At my expense.)

Not surprisingly, the response was minimal. I decided it was similar to the instruction on a pack of cigarettes, *The contents can be injurious to your health.* This booklet was injurious to their emotional health, so better to ignore it.

My brothers, the survival of our Jewish People can only be maintained by aliyah. Look at the statistics: What is the current rate of intermarriage? 50-60-70%. What is the percentage of affiliation to Jewish synagogues and institutions in the Diaspora?

The instructions are there for all to read. The continuance of the Diaspora will be injurious to the health of our Jewish People.

THE YOM KIPPUR WAR
PART I

As Yom Kippur 1973 arrived, I was again in the midst of a divorce, this time from Bea, after six years of marriage (covered in Marriage #2). We had attempted reconciliation, to no avail. My Kol Nidre night pre-fast meal was taken depressingly alone, and after the return walk from shul, I sat alone in my large home, my thoughts with my three children, dispersed along the eastern coast of America.

The morning radio alarm came on at 6 a.m. as usual. (My religious observance was typical Conservative American; Yom Kippur meant fast, perhaps walk to shul with a "High Holiday Clothes Consciousness".) The startling news report was that Israel was under attack on two fronts. I leaped out of bed, dressed quickly, and ran to deliver the news to our Rabbi Goldberg at the Hewlett-East Rockaway Conservative Jewish Center. I approached the bimah.[1]

J.M.: "Rabbi, I just heard a radio report; Israel has been attacked."

Rabbi: "There will be time to evaluate this after our services."

J.M.: "Shouldn't you inform the congregation at once?"

Rabbi: "I'll make a reference after my sermon."

And so it was...

After breaking the fast, I stayed up most of the night, listening to radio and TV situation reports. The TV proliferated with film of victorious Egyptian and

---

1. bimah – pulpit.

Syrian soldiers who had overrun Israeli fortifications. It showed our burnt-out tanks and the frenzied enemy soldiers dancing or burning Israeli flags.

In the morning I told my partners I could not go through the regimen of daily business activity, with Israel under such distress. I went on the phone and began to call friends and business associates to give financial support. We also made a good contribution. In total, I collected about $15-20,000. What shocked me, as I traveled around pleading for funds, was that many fellow-Jews were indifferent, some totally cold. Others told me they had made other charity commitments. I could not fathom this coming from Jews. On the third day, with little else to do personally, I did something on impulse, as is my usual modus operandi. I called my travel agent at Zenith Tours – Andy Pesky.

JM: "Andy, how can I get to Israel?"

AP: "Are you nuts? There is a war going on there."

JM: "Andy, as a friend, check out the possibilities of buying a ticket."

AP: "It's crazy, but I'll try, for you."

That afternoon:

AP: "Yes, I can get you on an El-Al flight, but only first class."

JM: "Book it! Just advise me when and where."

AP: "This is really ironic. I've never heard of someone going to war first class!"

That evening, with my reservations confirmed and my departure in two days, I called a meeting of my partners.

JM: "Cousins, I'm going to Israel to help our fellow Jews."

Partners: "And who will carry on your end in the time you're gone? Do you expect to be on salary? Maybe next time there will be a war in Brazil; will you also leave?" Plus many other negatives.

I departed that evening with the remark, "If I return, we can continue the arguments. If I don't, you can divide my equity among my dependents. I trust you'll do the fair thing."

The next morning I met with my old friend and attorney, Dave Ferdinand, z"l, to update my will and give some instructions. I advised Lisa and Mitchell of my plans (Jackie was too young), said goodbye to a number of relatives and friends, and took a taxi to JFK that evening. I carried only one small collapsible bag, mostly with outdoor clothes and boots, plus personal effects, including my

Zadah's siddur, tefillin, and his small 2"x3" photo (same as the dedication photo).

The Trip

In a separate waiting lounge, I found myself sitting among mainly returning Israelis, a number of American volunteers like myself, including Vietnam War vets, news people, and several other foreign adventurers. We were initially thoroughly screened by Israeli agents: "What do you plan to do in Israel Mr. Mink?"

"Anything I can to defend our homeland and assist our people."

Finally, after boarding, we sat on the tarmac for several hours, awaiting a VIP. When he finally arrived, it was Abba Eban, our foreign minister, who came directly from the U.N. debates. He and several aides joined me in the first class section. The flight was very tense, with no small talk. We landed first in Paris, where Mr. Eban and his entourage departed for several hours – we assumed on vital business. Finally, the Boeing 707 headed toward Tel Aviv, curtains drawn, in nearly complete darkness, entering the war zone.

THE YOM KIPPUR WAR
PART 2

Arrival

I suspect we all fantasize how events will transpire prior to their happening. To my surprise and disappointment, totally absent was a reception committee to direct us volunteers how to get involved in the war effort. The Tel Aviv Hilton was fully occupied with media people. The next morning, I left to buy sunglasses which I had forgotten to pack. As I left the hotel, I encountered two men my age, clearly Americans from their conversation. One turned out to be Murray Greenfield, an ex-American activist, and the second, Philip Cohen, I would encounter seven years later when I was employed by Bank Leumi.

JM: "Gentleman, tell me what I can do to help?"

MG: "Can you drive a truck?"

JM: "I've done it for years."

MG: "Go over to the Ministry of Transportation and ask to take a truck drivers test."

As instructed, I taxied there and with great difficulty explained my purpose in coming to Israel. At this point the clerk typically gave me a long form to fill out – all in Hebrew! When I explained my language deficiency, she replied, "Slicha (sorry). You must complete the form." Obviously a dead end.

Now let us backtrack to July 1968. On my first visit to Israel I met the Tamari family, who resided opposite the Tel Aviv Hilton. We had become friends. I had rented a car in '68, and together we had driven up north to visit the father's family, the Rosenbergs, in Kibbutz Ayelet Hashachar, in the lower

Galilee. We stayed at the kibbutz for several days and became close with the Rosenberg family as well. They were pioneers and founders living at the kibbutz for 30 years. My wife, Bayla, sent the Rosenbergs a gift in appreciation of their hospitality when we returned to the States.

The Shoshana Saga

As I write this autobiography, I see how a chain of events led to my decision to live permanently in Eretz Israel. I had met a young woman, Ilana Tamari, and her family on my first day in Israel in July, 1968. Again, on my first day in Israel during the Yom Kippur War, I visited the Tamaris. They were shocked to see me and again, together we drove up to the kibbutz, after I had rented a Volvo station wagon.

As we drove north, I was astounded by the countless hundreds of soldiers stranded on the roads in both directions. Public transport (Egged) had been suspended for the duration. Returning to Tel Aviv that evening with the Tamaris, we passed Rosh Pina, a town south of the kibbutz. Since there were a few seats available in the car, I opened the doors and offered a lift to several stranded soldiers. They jumped in at once, leaving dozens behind. That evening, as though by inspiration, I realized *there was* something I could do for the war effort. Next morning, I arose at 6 a.m., drove to a road junction in north Tel Aviv, and in my non-existent Hebrew yelled out, "Rosh Pina!" The car was quickly filled. The difficulty for me was my total lack of Hebrew; I simply followed hand signals for days on end with little or no conversation. On the Northern front, we were often able to drive into the war-torn city of Kuneitra (since returned to Syria). At times I found myself in military convoys. One evening, instead of returning to the Hilton, I stayed at Kibbutz Ayelet Hashachar again, suffering from total exhaustion. (P.S.: My exploits were covered in the New York Magazine.)

The next morning my hosts, Willy and Nussia Rosenberg (now both deceased), suggested that as I looked so worn out, I should stay on. They were very short of help at the kibbutz. I could spend a few days working there and thus get off the roads. I agreed, and was provided with a small hut to sleep in. In the morning, I was assigned to irrigating the grapefruit orchard. Several days later, Nussia suggested that I help in the kitchen. Unexpectedly, I met an American kibbutznik, not only from the States, but a graduate of Hunter College in New York City. At last, someone I could relate to. As we did the kitchen chores, we joked about our former lives in the States. Shoshana Weidenfeld was a Zionist. After graduating college, she came by ship to Israel and joined this Hashomer Hatzair kibbutz (non-religious and very left-wing). She met and married Zeev Weidenfeld and raised a family. That evening I told the Rosenbergs about my new-found friend, Shoshana.

Nussia R: "Jerry, didn't Shoshana tell you what happened?!? Last week, her oldest son, Ya'acov, was killed at the Syrian front."

I was in total disbelief and shock. How did Shoshana go on?

The next morning, I approached Shoshana in the kitchen with apologies and trepidation.

JM: "Shoshana, what can I say? The Rosenbergs told me last night about the loss of your oldest son, Ya'acov."

Shoshana: "I assumed that, Jerry. Don't be embarrassed or ashamed. You just weren't informed."

THE NEXT FEW LINES WERE PERHAPS A MAJOR TURNING-POINT IN MY LIFE.

JM: "Shoshana, how can you manage to carry on?"

Shoshana: "TRUTHFULLY, WHEN I DECIDED TO BECOME A FULLY COMMITTED ZIONIST AND MAKE ALIYAH, I EXPECTED IT TO BE HARD AND PAINFUL. IT WAS ONLY LAST WEEK I REALIZED HOW HARD AND PAINFUL IT WOULD BECOME."

I stood there frozen and began to cry openly before Shoshana. That evening, I paid a symbolic condolence call on the family. (Kibbutz members did not sit shiva.) I met Zeev Weidenfeld, a Shoah survivor from Rumania, and their other children. I was shown a 3"×4" photo of Ya'acov, z"l, on their living room table, and volunteered to have it enlarged and framed when I returned to the States. A duplicate of that photo has been with me for the past 23 years and hangs in my study here in Jerusalem today. At the low points in my aliyah (to be covered in subsequent chapters) I look at the photo and gain renewed strength.

In an effort to reconstruct the Shoshana saga correctly, on impulse I called telephone information here in Israel. Unbelievably, I found myself phoning Shoshana W. We had a memorable conversation after 23 years. She refreshed my memory with names and dates, and recently visited Jerusalem, where we met again.

There are *many* levels of pain and sacrifice, Shoshana said that day. Subconsciously I probably made a neder (promise) that I would also make my contribution with whatever it took to Zionism and Israel.

The phone system in Israel at that point, 1973, was totally inadequate. Perhaps a third of the population was connected. I experienced countless memorable reunions, with parents and loved ones, and witnessed, after driving them home, soldiers learning of the death or injury of their comrades. This is indescribable for me, a scribbler of memories, unable properly to record these scenes on paper.

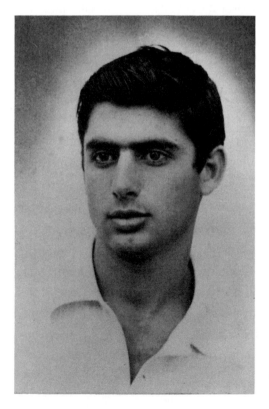

Yaakov Weidenfeld, who fell in the Yom Kippur War and inspired my aliyah

After the cessation of hostilities, I remained an additional week at the Hilton, TA, and visited the families of several soldiers I had chauffeured (English speakers). Most memorable, Danny Ofer, married to an American woman, Jeanie. Just about the time I made aliyah, Danny and family moved the opposite way, to Long Island. He found a job in his field – shoe salesman – in Great Neck, LI, prospered, and eventually moved to New Jersey. We now exchange Shana Tova greetings each year, but from opposite venues.

Another soldier was Dr. Dov Tamir. He was picked up on a dusty road near Kuneitra. He had been treating the wounded non-stop for many days, was dazed and exhausted. I had returned him to his home and wife, Nurit, and family in Rehovot.

Now, Jerry Mink decided it was also time to go home and pick up the threads of his life.

A LIBRARY IN MAMA'S MEMORY
AND A SEFER TORAH FOR ISRAEL

Having made the decision after the Yom Kippur War to get more involved in Israel, I was introduced to Moshe Golan in Tel Aviv. This was the first step in my resolve to create a 20th century scrap business in Israel. (Subject of the chapter HIL.)

This required a number of trips, first to investigate the possibilities and second, to decide how, where, and with how much of an investment. During one such trip (I probably made ten or more), I looked up my old friend, Rabbi Meyer Fendel, principal of HANC (Hebrew Academy of Nassau County), that my son Mitchell had attended.

One of the most memorable and tragic events had just occurred, which would become another painful milestone in our Israeli history – the Ma'alot Massacre. To recap this event: an outing had been arranged for a class of religious high school students from Safed, with an overnight sleepover in Ma'alot, a town on the Lebanese border. A gang of Arafat's henchmen (now called Palestine Authority policemen) massacred twenty-two children and their teachers.

On locating Rabbi Fendel (who was in Israel on a year's sabbatical), we arranged to go up north to the scene of the tragedy which had shocked the entire Jewish and civilized world. We arrived at a depressing sight: an old, decrepit building which served as the religious high school in Safad, with the attending students in psychological shock. I was moved, and was subsequently introduced to the principal. I inquired as to what I could do. He pointed out that their library desperately needed major improvement, books as well as facilities for studying. I established a fund for this purpose, and when they moved to a new building sponsored by a British benefactor, I enlarged the fund considerably. Years later, a beautiful new library was named and dedicated in memory of my beloved mother, Chaya Leah Mink.

A Torah for Israel

During that visit to Safad, I also met with the Yemenite father of a young soldier who had fallen in the Yom Kippur War. As a religious man, he desperately wanted to acquire a Sefer Torah in his fallen son's name. I committed myself to supply a Torah.

I knew as much about buying a Sefer Torah as I did about flying a jet fighter plane. I returned shortly to the States on a new mission. The only contact I had with the serious, religious world at that point was a Rabbi P_____, who had called on us for years, first on my father and then on me, for tzedaka (charity) several times a year. The rabbi had this great line when he came in, "Nu Mr. Mink, how is business?" If you said good, his reply was, "Give tzedaka; it will remain good." If you said bad, he replied, "You want it to get better? Give tzedaka!"

I found one of his receipts and made contact. Needless to say, the rabbi was astounded that I was calling him. I explained my predicament. He responded, "Leave everything to me, Mr. Mink!" When he came to my office and informed me that a new Sefer Torah would cost more than $10,000, I asked if a second-hand one could be found. In a few weeks I received an urgent call – Rabbi P_____ had located a wonderful used Sefer Torah for sale. We arranged a hurried meeting at my office. He arrived accompanied by another Orthodox gentleman. They had found a second-hand Torah in excellent condition, for sale, cash on the line; our negotiations were swift. We hondled[1] for five minutes and came up with a mutually agreed price for the perfect, used Torah.

Within a few days, Rabbi P_____ and colleague were at my office again. I was overwhelmed that I now owned a Torah. But now what to do with it after paying the rabbi? I locked it in the conference room (a new Aron Kodesh –

---

1. hondled – bargained.

literally, holy closet for the Torah) with instructions that no one was to enter. I took it home that evening and had my current girlfriend sew up a bed sheet as a covering. Within a week, I was again flying to Israel. After clearing security, wearing a kippa (head covering) for the entire twelve-hour trip (a first for me), the Torah in my lap, I arrived in Israel at my regular residence, the Hilton, Tel Aviv, and called Rabbi Fendel.

We arranged a ceremony the next day. A functionary from the Ministry of Religion, Rabbi Eliyahu Marcus, arrived; pictures were taken of the handing over the Torah ceremony: Jerry Mink to Rabbi Marcus to Father of Fallen Soldier. L'chaims were exchanged and drunk. The best and worst were yet to come. Several days later, a harried Rabbi Fendel called me: "We must meet at once!" The story: The Torah was pussel[1]! This was a new word in my non-existent religious lexicon. "What does pussel mean?" I asked. It seems the Torah had been kept for an extended period in a damp environment. Therefore, the letters were rising, separating from the parchment, and chipping off, thus rendering the Torah pussel and unusable.

Immediately I called my office on Long Island, which contacted Rabbi P_____. The balance is loshen hora. Yes, I did recover a major part of my money, which I gave to the father of the fallen soldier to make a purchase himself. Rabbi Fendel brought the Torah on his return trip to the States several months later. It was returned to Rabbi P_____, who extended thousands of apologies.

Sometimes, it's so difficult to do a mitzvah (good deed). But as Rabbi Mordechai Goldstein of the Diaspora Yeshiva always says, "If mitzvahs were that easy, everyone would do them."

---

1. pussel – not kosher according to Jewish Law.

ONLY IN ISRAEL
#1

Upon making aliyah in 1976, I was advised to promptly purchase an expensive car and exercise my rights as a new immigrant. I purchased a luxury Alpha Romeo model GTV. It was stolen three times and recovered each time by the police at various locations. Prior to the Camp David Agreement and the Palestine Authority, the thieves had nowhere to escape since the borders were sealed tight.

As luck would have it, my shining new car was run into while parked. I quickly found a body repair shop and arranged for the necessary repair. Within two weeks I was summmoned to the shop to redeem my car. On receiving the bill, I was shocked to note it was 50% more than agreed upon.

YM, American freyer[1]: "This is 50% more than we agreed upon."

Shop owner: "The sign in front says poch (body work) painting is an extra charge. Plus, of course, 18% VAT, etc., etc."

Lesson #154 was well learned. On entering a body shop with the Mink-mobile I now request the total price – all included.

---

1. freyer – sucker.

THE ISRAELI GUILT TRIP

I have concluded that it is unfair to blame only Jewish mothers who supposedly involve us in guilt trips. But, rather, there is a portion in our genetic make-up that forces the Jew to carry the burden of guilt. (Perhaps it is even carried forward from our experiences in the desert, e.g., Moshe and the Golden Calf at Sinai.)

Allow me to review several of my experiences and to partially explain how and why I now call myself stupid.

My initial meetings with both Moshe Golan and Aviva Ranani were embellished by tales of suffering they had experienced in the early years before and after the state was declared. Golan survived World War II as a Jew in Munkacs, Hungary, by stealth and instinct. Arrived in Israel after the war as a refugee; was deposited on a beach; lived with his wife in a tent, totally bereft of possesssions; one egg a week per family, etc., etc. Aviva, huddled in a bomb shelter as a child in Tel Aviv; desperate conditions during the war years. Could these people of sacrifice for Am Israel be anything but good?

In retrospect, the vast majority was heroic. But the Golans and Rananis used their experiences as tools for a guilt trip advantage. I was forced to question myself. How could I have allowed myself – a fellow-Jew – to live in safety and various degrees of luxury while they were experiencing such deprivation. It was not a level playing field. So, in remorse and guilt, you unshackle yourself from common sense and protective layers of armor and allow these viruses to invade; allow them access to your *valuables* and *trust*. Imagine the hardened American businessman, Jerry Mink, giving total power of attorney on a $75,000 deposit to an uninvestigated stranger, Moshe Golan, even after being forewarned by his former partner. Or Aviva coming forward with a tale of an abusing husband, etc., and demanding to investigate the American freyer!?

To epitomize these guilt trip stories, here is an example.

On arriving in Israel, during the first week of the Yom Kippur War (covered in another chapter), I found myself without sunglasses. I left the hotel early the first morning and began walking up Dizengoff Blvd. looking for an optometrist. On entering the shop, I found a teenage girl negotiating with the shopkeeper on the purchase, also, of sunglasses.

Fortunately, the optometrist spoke English. I inquired as to the goings on. He replied, "This young lady wishes to buy sunglasses for her brother who is in the Sinai, at the front." I immediately beseeched him, "I'll pay for the glasses." He asked why. The young lady thought my intentions were unfathomable (an act of seduction between this grandfather and a teenager?). It's irrelevant, but I bought the glasses for her soldier brother and myself and left both of them confused. It's evident I was guilt-laden and in desperate need to unburden myself by means of a commodity I had in oversupply at that time – money. There have been many other events.

ONLY IN ISRAEL
#2

Later, I related a tale of at last finding an honorable businessman here in Israel after many disappointments. This was Dr. Eli Adler, of Edmonton, Alberta, Canada. He had purchased my Neve Avivim penthouse and most of my furnishings. The deal was made on a handshake, without problems or "I thought you meant" distortions.

Once Eli arrived with the intention of residing here on a part-time basis with his family, he purchased a fourth hand VW Beetle. Similar to my experience 18 years later, the engine number did not correspond to its registration number. To a Western emigre, "What the heck's the difference," but not to the multi-tiered bureaucratic hierarchy.

Bureaucrat: "Dr. Adler, why did you change the engine?"

Adler: "I didn't change it; I purchased it that way."

Bureaucrat: "We have had numerous cases of old VW's now being 'souped-up' with high powered engines, changing their taxation value."

Adler: "I assure you I am not a 'hot rod' enthusiast. I purchased this small car merely to run local errands."

Bureaucrat: "Well, Dr. Adler, if you want this car registered you will have to bring verification from an *"automotive engineer,"* preferably a Technion graduate, who can certify the *real* H.P. of your Beetle engine."

Adler: "That's ridiculous!"

Bureaucrat: "You will not pull the wool over our eyes."

Adler now realized what it means to be a Zionist in Israel, as opposed to Zionism as practiced in Canada.

Yes, he found an engine mumcha[1] who charged him several hundred dollars to remove the heads, measure the diameter of the pistons, reseal the engine, and supply a certificate. And just like that, Eli was able to acquire a license for this fourth hand VW.

---

1. mumcha – expert.

THE MIFROMAL EXPERIENCE

As you enter Har Nof, a neighborhood in Jerusalem, on either side there is significant ongoing construction of a commercial and industrial park being developed. The largest factory is Mifromal, a metal extruding plant for aluminum and brass. I believe it is privately held. The summer of 1973 Cousins Metal was contacted by a broker (Martha Light), a common practice. "I have an exporter looking for rod brass chips, industry, code name *Night*." We were quoted a price; after some back and forth we agreed to the terms – 20 tons packed in 55-gallon sealed drums, to be delivered in a sea-going container on instructions. The buyer was Phillips Brothers (the Jesselson firm). On receiving the contract and instructions, we were surprised to see the destination was Ashdod, Israel. The ensuing tale is somewhat historic; just at the point we were about to make shipment, the Yom Kippur war broke out. The buyer called us and said we could reject the contract since force majeure had taken place. This is an international understanding covering natural disasters, wars, massive labor disputes, and other unforeseeables. We volunteered to put the material aside and wait for events to develop. I like to think, in a small way, it was our war effort contribution. I departed for my volunteer effort in Israel. Several months later, we were notified by Phillips Bros. that they would now accept shipment.

Unbelievably, about six months later, I visited the Mifromal factory with my future partner, Moshe Golan. There, sitting in the stockpile of scrap to be processed, was the CMI shipment. Strange; may I suggest Divine Intervention?

ONLY IN ISRAEL
#3

My friend Mike Kramer had asked me to drive him downtown to pick up a package on Jaffa Road. I stopped for two minutes on Jaffa Road while he ran into the shop. When he emerged, I jumped out to open the trunk, and then we both hopped back into the car. We had gone some 20 or 30 meters when a policewoman pulled us over for not resecuring our safety belts. I argued vehemently but to no avail. I chose to enter a plea of "not guilty." Some eight months later the case went to trial. When our case was finally called, I faced a kippa-clad judge, with my star witness Kramer at my side.

The judge looked down on the two kippa-covered middle-aged men in front of his bench, and the following conversation ensued between us:

Judge: Do you speak Hebrew, English or Yiddish?

Me: Broken Hebrew, your Honor.

Judge: Let's hear your story.

(I then proceeded to explain the circumstances as best I could.)

Judge: You're sure you drove only 20 or 30 meters?

Me: Positive, your Honor.

Judge: So you're an expert on distances?

Me: I think so.

Judge: How high should the water be in a mikva[1] to make it kosher?

Me: (I looked at Kramer. We both shrugged.) I don't know.

Judge: An expert on lengths would know it's one and a half cubits.

---

1. mikva –ceremonial pool or bath.

Me: What's the connection?

Judge: This proves you know very little about lengths. The fine is 100 shekels.

Me: But your Honor...

Judge: No "buts." The usual fine is 280 NIS. I'm letting you off easy. Better you should sit and learn Gemora than to drive around town like an errand boy – case closed!

(This story is as it appeared in "Your Jerusalem" 1995)

HOW TO LOSE
A MILLION 1996 DOLLARS

Part I

Returning from my Yom Kippur War saga, my Zionist zeal was overpowering; but, how to exercise it? A friend and business associate, Mel Dubin, President of Slant Fan Manufacturing on Long Island, phoned me. "I'm assembling a group of like-minded good Jews and Zionists on a project. Please join us!"

Simply stated, 20 businessmen invested $5,000 each to initiate a firm whose purpose was to import Israeli-manufactured goods. Remember, this is 1974, a time when Israel was known only for exporting oranges and hard luck stories.

Mel is a gentleman, and committed American Zionist. Several years before he had established a division of his baseboard heating business in Ashdod, Israel, and was succeeding in taking only a small loss yearly, which his successful L.I. firm was easily able to absorb.

The enthusiastic group was introduced to two Israelis, who would operate the new firm in Mel's Long Island office: thus, no phone, office, or secretarial service expenses. What a guy! Each of us was introduced to the Israeli operators. We explained our business activities, and inquired how we could be of assistance. I was at the lowest rung – a scrap dealer. At this crucial point, one of the Israelis said, "I know someone in the scrap business in Israel who I'm certain would be pleased to meet you." (This should be followed by somber music!)

Back to our story. Six months passed. I paid little attention to the new Israeli venture after investing our $5,000. Mel Dubin called again. We need a board of directors meeting of our new firm ASAP. Please be at my office at this time and date.

Bottom Line – The original $5,000 ante was exhausted on various traveling expenses and salaries. To continue, we would have to come up with an additional $3,500 each. Now I had to go back and relate this to my partners, who were less than enthusiastic about the original idea.

It was a tough sell. I received instructions from them to find out what happened to the original $100,000. I called the management team, made inquiries as to how *I* could help. What can they supply for business and profit? They showed me several products, including a small metal box – a simple sheet steel box with electro spot welds on each corner – which one of their Israeli suppliers could provide.

Michael Wahl, a friend with a factory in L.I. City, made display items and tchatkes.[1] I showed Michael the sample made in Israel.

Mike: "How many can they make and how much do they want?" I ran back to their office: "Can you make these in volume?" "Yes." "How much will it cost landed in New York?" "$1.25 each." Said Michael: "You have an order, but I'm willing to pay $1.50 each! As another good Jew that's my contribution!" I brought the order back to Expeditors, contracts signed, telexes sent – a volume business, finally. *Bottom Line* – Delivery not on time; Michael Wahl angry; Jerry Mink, the idiot, $8,500 in minus.

But I had an Israeli scrap dealer contact in Israel; a bad omen.

---

1. tchatkes – knick-knacks.

BIALYSTOK REVISITED

We are seated at the home of my favorite cousins, Drs. Jack and Nicole Kerman, and their daughter, Robin. The annual Thanksgiving Dinner has been almost a ritual for the past 15 years. (Referred to later in the BatSheva chapter.) The conversation wandered into the roots of the Gering (a.k.a. Blumberg) family tree. I asked myself, why hadn't I returned to my forebears' home?

Like most American Jews, I could only trace my roots for two or three generations, at best. My maternal family history was based on Grandfather Nahum Haim Gering and my Grandmother Shoshana. I was given the name Yechezkel after her father, my great-grandfather. The surname *Gering* suggests that at some point the family resided in Germany, having probably gotten there via the Iberian Peninsula following the Spanish Inquistion. We are all dark-eyed and black haired. However, this is all supposition, and not historical fact. On my father's side, the story seems to be: Shlomo Yehuda Minkowitz was married twice, I'm certain. His older children were taller and bigger-boned than my father and his younger sister, Chaika. Again, all this is based on observation and assumption. My sister, Selma (Shana) was named after my father's mother, the second wife.

At my first opportunity, I called travel agent Andy Pesky, of Yom Kippur War history notoriety.

JM: "Andy, I want to trace my ancestry in Bialystok, Poland. Arrange a flight and hotel reservations."

AP: "What's Bialystok?"

JM: "You know, like the 'bialy' (onion roll) you probably eat Sunday morning. Bialy is a nickname for Bialystoker Kuchens (a type of breadroll)."

AP: "You're too much, Jerry, but I'll check it out, anyway."

Several days later...

AP: "Jerry, there is no Bialystok Airport, period. Also, there is no hotel. The Polish embassy, which was quite hostile, replied there is only a one-star inn in Bialystok. The best I can do for flight arrangements for you is to go via Israel. (I was in the midst of creating the I.R.C. disaster in 1974. See chapter: How to Lose a Million 1996 Dollars.) You can fly Tel Aviv – Bucharest, Romania with Tarom; then Bucharest to Prague, Czecheslovakia, and Prague to Warsaw. From there, take a train to Bialystok and return by train to Warsaw. And Jerry, remember, this is all behind the Iron Curtain. I think you're crazy, but again, what can I say?" (The return leg was Warsaw to Amsterdam by KLM, and on to New York.)

JM: "Book it!!"

Historical Perspective

In 1982, a successful member of the Bialystok Landsleit (Former Resident Society), Max Ratner, an industrialist and philanthropist founder of Forest City Enterprises of Cleveland, Ohio, USA, subsidized the composition and publication of a Bialystoker Memorial Book. Ratner, strangely enough, came to the USA in the same year as my dear mother, 1920. From this almanac I gathered the following facts:

> Bialystok in Polish means "white river".
>
> The city was established in 1320. The Jews were invited during the 16th century, and it soon became a center of silk and cotton textile manufacturing, thanks to its Jewish population. However, Bialystok was best known as a center for Torah study and tzedaka.
>
> Statistics: By the 19th century, it was 64% Jewish. Prior to the German invasion in 1940, the total population stood at

100,000 – approximately 60,000 were Jewish. By 1982, the population was 268,000; the number of Jews – 7!

The Memorable Trip

I arrived in Warsaw after being body-searched in Prague. I took a cab from the airport to the central train station. The 2½ hour trip by first class coach to Bialystok cost $1.30. The return ride via regular coach was $0.80. However, that took 4 hours.

As I had done previously on the trip to Russia to check out Papa's "menu," I first contacted a local New York authority. In this case, it was the Bialystok Home for the Aged at 228 East Broadway, New York City. The Gering (Blumberg) family, including my beloved mother, had been supporters and benefactors of this Manhattan institution for countless years. The administrator at the time, Mr. Itzak Rybal, was an old friend.

Visiting Bialystok (and freezing), 1974

When he heard of my intentions, he supplied me with names and and addresses of six or eight Jews to contact. The Bialystoker organization had maintained contact with them since the end of the Shoah, all now advanced in age, desperately poor, and in failing health. They were being supplied with some basic medicines and holiday period financial aid.

The Arrival

To assign the Bialystok "Hilton" a single star was overly generous. On checking in, "yes, they had my reservation." The luggage was walked up by a lady porter, who appeared capable of carrying me also. The room could better be called a 6×10-foot cell. It consisted of 1 cot, 1 chest of drawers (metal), 1 sink – cold water only, 1 chair, and the toilet down the hall was available for all 30 rooms in my wing. The plumbing was beyond description, and revolting. The floor I was on was built at a 90 degree angle, 30 rooms on each leg. A wardress, as she appeared to me, sat at the corner table so she could observe all 60 rooms. There was no lock on the door. At night I pushed the dresser against the door for some level of security. The other occupants appeared to be mostly Polish army officers. It has been more than 23 years since the visit; the one thing I clearly recall is that I was *never* again as cold as those three days and nights in Bialystok. There was no thought of changing my clothes, inner or outer. I went about and slept in the same outfit. That first evening, I located via taxi the first poor soul, who resided in a laborers' housing complex. He arranged for us to meet the other six Jewish survivors.

The next morning, I came down stiff with cold and I treated them to breakfast. I related in Yiddish my intention to locate my Zadah's burial place. I planned to take a cab out to the cemetery. They objected: "Why waste the money? The open trolley (no windows or doors) goes the same way."

I found it next to impossible to communicate. They thought they were speaking Yiddish; in reality, their Yiddish was now 50% or more Polish, from years of disuse. My hands and feet were still frozen from the night before. But they insisted on the trolley ride. It was a maddeningly cold half hour trip. When we arrived, I found the cemetery in total disarray. It had been untended for the past 35 years. Snow and overgrown weeds covered the approximately five-acre site. I thought that by some miracle I would find my grandparents' burial site, but the miracle did not occur, even after trudging through endless rows of inscribed stones. Now totally numb from the cold, I capitulated and gave up my search. The four of us walked back to the trolley station, eventually returning to the inn. That night, they brought their families. All had survived the war and thereafter by intermarriage. We had a meal together (for me, inedible). The next day, they all came with pockets full of Polish zlotys to exchange for US dollars. I recognized their simple scam; but in an effort to assist them, I converted several hundred US dollars into local currency. I couldn't spend all the zlotys if I stayed a month. The following day we went "sight-seeing."

The sights were tragic beyond description. They pointed out: Here was the main Jewish ghetto, totally destroyed in the Bialystok Uprising in August, 1943 against the Nazis (similar to the Warsaw Ghetto uprising). There stood the main synagogue, burned to the ground, together with 2,000 Jewish souls inside. At various locations were plaques and minor memorial pillars to the slaughtered thousands of my kinsfolk. It was devastating and living proof of the barbarity of the German people, whose grand plan was to eliminate any trace of our heritage from this world.

After three days of a tea, bread and cake diet, freezing day and night, without washing or bathroom facilities, it was time to return to civilization. I said goodbye to these seven impoverished Jewish souls and made a promise that their basic needs would continue to be supplied via the Bialystoker New York organization – I set up a fund on my return to New York – and took the train to Warsaw.

The Warsaw Experience

Not to be overly melodramatic, after the four-hour train ride to Warsaw, I was suddenly transferred from a 17th century hovel to 20th century accommodations. Andy Pesky had reserved a room in a new Scandinavian 'turn-key' (ready for occupancy) constructed hotel. Light, heat, a bed, a hot shower: I stood in it for fifteen minutes to thaw out. Then only I put on a fresh outfit and realized I was very hungry. Washed, dressed and relaxed, I went down to the dining room.

Maitre de: "Sir, are you alone?'

JM: "Yes. I'm a tourist."

Maitre de: "Would you like to join another traveler?"

JM: "Certainly, why not."

I was escorted to a table, and introduced to a businessman. At once, I discovered he was a German, about my age.

German: "Where have you come from?"

JM: "I'm an American Jew and I just returned from Bialystok."

German: "Yes, I know the city; I sell dental equipment and supplies out of Dresden (East Germany at the time). I travel there several times a year. How did you like the city?"

JM: "There was nothing to like. I came searching for my ancestral roots in what was once a center of Jewish culture and learning for about 60,000 Jews. You know how many I found there? *Seven Jews!!* Tell me,

HOW COULD YOUR PEOPLE HAVE DONE THIS TO MY PEOPLE?"

With each word, my pent-up emotions were rising. The German S.O.B. recognized it also. I say this now, unemotionally, but I'm certain if he had given me a nasty or negative response, I would have put a knife through his heart, regardless of the consequences. Now, obviously distressed, he looked at me very hard, got up, semi-bowed and left the table without another word.

Thus my pilgrimage to Bialystok ended in remorse and rage and was somewhat fruitless. I returned the next day to the USA.

THE MILLION DOLLAR FIASCO

Allow me first to quote one of my idols from the 1950's, Adlaï Stevenson, who ran for President as a Democrat in 1952 and 1956, losing badly to Ike on both occasions. He was quoting a statement made 100 years earlier by Abe Lincoln, the 16th president of the USA. "I'm too big to cry, but old enough to know that it hurts."

Several of the names escape me after 20 years, but the events remain crystal clear.

One of the principals in the soon to expire Israeli Products Sales Company on Long Island suggested I might wish to meet the Israeli gentleman, then living in New York, who had made an investment with a Moshe Golan and Haim Golan (not related). The three partners had purchased the property from the Histradrut, together with a smelter and a warehouse facility, located in the Ashdod Industrial area, close to the port. Ashdod Metal Refining, on 16 dunams (4 acres), with an impressive two-story concrete building plus a $300,000 carried forward loss.

The New York Israeli and Haim Golan wanted out. I met one partner in New York, the Israeli, who outlined why he wanted to sell. (He was now living in New York.) I met the Golans in Tel Aviv and quickly struck a deal.

The shocking part was, as Haim was leaving for Zurich, Switzerland, where he permanently resided, he invited me for tea one afternoon. After some small talk, he took me by the hand and said, "You are an American whose intentions are honest. Just one word: Do not go into business with Moshe Golan!" I responded, "Haim, this is against your own best interests. Why?" He repeated his warning again, with no commentary. "Do not go into business with Moshe Golan." We parted. I don't believe I saw him again, since everything thereafter was handled by attorneys.

Was this another case of Divine Intervention? But this time, foolishly not heeded.

IRC (HIL) AND YOSSI ANGEL

At this point, after signing the agreement to purchase half the Ashdod property, I offered the deal to my partners in the States, my cousins, the Gering brothers. Our relationship had deteriorated, especially after I had left on three days notice to volunteer in Israel during the Yom Kippur War. So I went it alone, driven by my all-consuming Zionist bent.

I had made a significant and very profitable contact in Europe to sell a specialty scrap, which necessitated my travelling back and forth, with a U-turn through Israel. Now that we had the property, my dream of establishing a 20th century scrap facility in Israel was on the way to becoming a fact on the ground. At this point, Moshe Golan introduced me to his son-in-law, Yossi Angel (a nephew of Danny Angel, of the bakery clan). Yossi had graduated university and married Moshe Golan's daughter. When the Yom Kippur War broke out, Yossi, an officer, was seriously wounded by shrapnel and had lost an eye. Moshe suggested that since I was forming a new venture on our jointly owned property, I might take Yossi in as an employee, teach him the scrap business, and as a patriot, help a wounded soldier. The request was irresistible.

Hence began the steps:

1. We formed a corporation, H.I.L. (Hevra Israel Lemichzur) or Israel Recycling Company. My expense.
2. I invited Yossi Angel to join me at Cousins Metal (in America) and learn the basics of operating a scrap business. My expense.
3. I purchased three used Mack container trucks and shipped them to Israel. My expense.

4. I purchased 54 disassembled containers and put them in sea-going containers. When assembled in our plant in Ashdod, people involved in industry came from all points to investigate this innovation, a first in Israel. My expense.
5. I purchased a hydraulic press for briquetting scrap steel, from Europe and shipped it to Israel. My expense.
6. I purchased, in Austria, a new large shear to cut steel sections and shipped it to Israel. My expense.
7. I purchased a used crane and electro magnet in Israel. My expense.
8. I purchased a smaller crane (Manof) with a grapple. My expense.
9. Etc., etc., etc. My expense.

In short order, property and all, I had invested over $350,000. It should be recalled that 1996 dollars are about 3 to 1 of 1976 dollars. In other words, by that point I had invested in the project an equivalent of one million at 1996 dollars.

Now began the downers:

There was $75,000 deposited at a Barclay's Discount Bank branch in Tel Aviv for working capital. Moshe Golan suggested I give him power of attorney over the account since I needed a rep in Israel (prior to my aliyah) to deal with company expenses. On my arrival, I discovered to my distress that Golan had used my power of attorney to extend himself a line of credit based on *my* $75,000. I was shocked. He freed the money up after some months.

Second, although Yossi Angel spent a month with me in the States observing and being instructed and coached, he was a sweet, honest nonstarter. I came to Moshe Golan with my complaint. He agreed Yossi Angel was not cut out for the scrap business. We requested his resignation, which he readily tendered.

Now, the disasters were coming fast and furiously. After quickly going through the $75,000 in Barclay's Bank, I applied for a line of credit, showing the bank management a total list of all my investments to date. Their response, "What are we going to do with this pile of iron (the equipment and trucks) if you go broke?" This was the general response in several other banks, as well.

Remember again, this is 1976-7. The only collateral they would accept was cash, foreign currency deposits, or securities.

In my agreement to sell my equity in Cousins Metal, I took a small amount of cash (spent on my apartment in Neve Avivim) and a series of notes for 10 years. My other property and rental income would be needed to pay alimony and child support. When presented to bankers here, they rejected the notes – (how will we collect our money *when you go broke?*). Not very encouraging. Without working capital, I raced back to New York, and found a friendly banker, David Crohn, at Bank Leumi, New York City. (He would eventually become my boss in Bank Leumi, Jerusalem.) The bank (for a fee), took the Cousins Metal promissory notes and issued a guarantee to Barclay's in Tel Aviv. With this, Barclay's extended me credits for $150,000, which is the amount I owed them when I was forced to close the business a year later.

I'm sure this sounds very complicated, but think how I felt watching my life's accumulated wealth slowly and uncontrollably go down the drain.

WIFE #3 AVIVA
PART I

Aviva Ranani

Just thinking about all these experiences is exhausting, but it is necessary to fit them all into the matrix as I tell my story.

I had been divorced from Bea (Bayla) about three years and travelled often to Israel, forming the ill-fated business venture, Israeli Recycling Company. On one such trip, I was introduced to Aviva, a practicing lawyer in Tel Aviv.

The Aviva story:

1. She had grown up as a single child in Tel Aviv in a very poor family. True.
2. She had a daughter from a previous marriage, Pia, a charming girl, now an M.D. (I have heard). True.
3. She was divorced from Dov Ranani. He was now remarried and living in Canada. True.

We began seeing each other on trips, as I was regularly returning to Israel. Aviva was very charming when need be, and assertive. The history of her divorce was total fabrication. Also, the tale of her ex-husband being a successful businessman. There was a slight omission for the period he spent in jail for defrauding a Swiss investor in a business venture. Also how Dov Ranani had sued her for divorce based on her infidelity; a minor oversight! But the major item on our agenda was: who is this Jerry Mink, already twice divorced, and why would he want or need to make aliyah? Well, there was no other recourse. I invited Aviva to New York and ensconced her in a major midtown hotel. She claimed to be a very successful Tel Aviv attorney. But when I saw her wardrobe,

I asked my cousin, Anita Reiner, to take her shopping. My business activities in the States were very profitable; no shortage of cash, despite paying two alimonies and child support for three children. First I introduced her to my family, friends and children and so on. Now came the climax. She demanded to know why I had divorced twice. (I was unaware of her forays.) I therefore arranged for two meetings, first with Gloria, then Bea. Gloria agreed to meet. (We had been divorced some ten years at this point.) We met Gloria at her home on Long Island. Introductions were made. The next thirty minutes was one continual tirade of accumulated rage and venom by Gloria. I never said a word. Aviva was in total shock. On departing, I realized that since I asked for the visit, I had no recourse. But I did remark to Gloria, "I hope at some point, if you introduce me to a gentleman whom you are involved with, I will act with better decorum and class. After all, I am the father of your two children."

I took Aviva back to her hotel in total silence. The next day, when I called her, she said she still wanted to meet Bea, to reconfirm Gloria's rage. I must admit Bea was a perfect lady and responded, "We divorced due to many irreconcilable differences."

Aviva accepted an engagement ring conditionally. She would have to reevaluate the entire visit, and what she had seen and heard, when she returned home (with suitcases full of goodies). She finally acquiesced to marriage, but after I made aliyah. During my next to last trip, she insisted we search for an apartment to purchase. Her apartment was inadequate for the newly arrived American millionaire.

I should have known it was a horrible mistake, but after spending three or four years in the New York City singles scene, I honestly dreamed of settling down, having a business career in Israel and beginning my life anew as an Israeli. I arranged a grand wedding reception around the outdoor pool at the Tel Aviv Hilton. Aviva invited everyone she even vaguely knew. We were now married. It should be noted that she always kept me on edge, even until the last day; should she or shouldn't she. We were formally married in the home of Rabbi Israel Lau, now chief Ashkenazi rabbi of Israel. I didn't know until she actually arrived at the rabbi's home if we were to be married that day.

Great hindsight, you idiot.

THE PENTHOUSE APARTMENT IN NEVE AVIVIM
ON OPPENHEIMER STREET, TEL AVIV

In 1976, the economy in Israel was in the doldrums. Aviva decided we had to buy an apartment, fitting for her new married life style.

She eventually located the twelfth floor penthouse in Neve Avivim. 280 meters, encircled by terraces, air conditioned, with an unbelievable view of the Mediterranean, but somewhat depressing and unlived in for several years. An Israeli couple had purchased it with the intention of returning to Israel from their shmatta business in Munich, Germany. At the outbreak of the Yom Kippur War, they were in the midst of upgrading a new apartment to their standards. The low morale and financial depression after the war changed their minds. In truth, I stole it for $155,000. I spent $25,000 for appliances, carpeting, and some carpentry and furniture. Aviva continuously informed me of the money she was saving us, since she was acting as the lawyer and decorator's assistant (to be noted later).

Some incidental information:

Yael Dayan (at that point a writer and publicist) and many Israeli heavyweights resided in this building. The identical apartment (the building had a twin) on Rechov Oppenheimer, is occupied, till today, by Shimon Peres.

THE AVIVA STORY CONTINUES

After a short honeymoon and buying trip to the States, we returned to resume a normal family life (I thought). On arrival in Israel, just prior to the marriage, I had purchased a used car and, at the same time, employing my immigrant rights, ordered a special Model Alpha Romeo GTV, which could take six months to arrive. It was at that point I discovered the deceit of Moshe Golan, my Israeli partner. In attempting to withdraw money to pay for the used car and the deposit for the new one, I was informed by the bank that my funds had been frozen to guarantee Golan's business activities. On confrontation, Golan said *he* would loan me money till mine was freed up (after a few months). I was furious and disappointed at this turn of events. Next, we moved Aviva's and her daughter's belongings from her old apartment to Neve Avivim. I suggested to Aviva to sell the place. Her reply, "That's not done in Israel." It was to be for Pia when she married. Pia was 15 at the time. O.K. "Rent it for several years." Also no good. Why not? No response. Within two or three months, a trivial argument arose. Aviva promptly moved back to her old apartment. In distress, I begged her to return. "Yes," she replied, "if you sign over your used car (to me) when the new one arrives." I agreed. A month or so passed and another minor disagreement; again she moved out. Again I appealed. She did not like the furnishings I had shipped in my container. "It was 'alta shmattas' (old rags) that people in Tel Aviv had thrown out years ago." In reality, it was a valuable collection of antique, restored furniture and paintings I had accumulated over time. I would have to get rid of it. In its place, she purchased Israeli second-class imitations of Western furnishings. I was forced to sell my collection to Israeli dealers at a fraction of its worth, after having paid to have it transported to Israel.

Suddenly, a new revelation! Aviva did not like Americans and their values and mannerisms. When questioned about who she thought I was, she replied, "Living with an American is different from shopping in New York."

An aside: When arranging the wedding, we required invitations. Aviva chose one with birds, flowers and multi-colored decorative symbols. I suggested a single gold, white and black design. This also caused a battle. In fact, Akiva and Ruth Federbush, the printers (who ultimately became my friends), had decided then and there that the marriage was doomed. They had never witnessed such a fight prior to a marriage. We had to leave the print shop and argue outside. (P.S. We took the birds, etc.)

The Final Breakup

I had assumed that living in Israel meant Jewish tradition. Aviva never lit candles; the religious holidays she spent all day in bed. On her return to work at her office, she demanded we hire a full-time maid. The two trips to the States and the wedding, buying an apartment and decorating it, had destroyed her practice, a statement that would be repeated daily during the entire time we were living together. We hired a full-time maid; within a few months, several came and departed, each worse than the previous one. Finally, she settled on Shoshana, an uneducated, unkempt young woman.

Coming home one afternoon earlier than usual, I found Shoshana entertaining her friends with lunch, plus playing with Pia's dog on the kitchen table. First, I pulled the dog by the leash off the table, and then asked Shoshana's lunch guests to leave at once. When Aviva arrived home that evening, Shoshana went on the offensive; I had embarrassed her and beaten Pia's dog (a lie). Aviva was irreconcilable, and the next day she packed and left for the third or fourth time for her old apartment, this time for good.

Within a week, I was served with a summons to appear in court for the purpose of a legal separation and eventual divorce. As with Papa's second wife, Pauline, it appeared everything had previously been put in place. I called her attorney, Dov Israeli, who dealt with her first divorce. "Mr. Israeli, I can't understand the grounds for this divorce, after six months of marriage." The following is unbelievable but true.

Attorney Israeli: "Mr. Mink, please come up to my office. Let's see what we can sort out."

Like an *idiot*, I complied. He suggested that prior to the office visit I write up a review of the events leading to this break-up. I constructed a 16-page summary of my history, aliyah, our meeting, marriage and our areas of disagreement and gave it to Israeli. He accepted *my* papers, told me he would review the information, and then went about dissecting it, taking words out of context, and using my statements for his case in court. I'm certain this was all unethical and illegal. A duplicate of my statement is in my files.

I was in for far more startling revelations. First, her papers accused me of physical and mental cruelty – lies. Second, she demanded I vacate *"her"* apartment. Remember, Aviva had done all the legal work. She had registered herself as co-owner. When questioned on this misappropriation of ownership, Aviva responded, "Do you think I would have married you without the apartment ownership?"

My Hebrew comprehension at that point was zero. I had an agency translate the papers and decided I needed no defense, since there was no basis after living together six months in an on and off course. I appeared alone; when the case was called, I immediately informed the judge there was a language barrier; also, I felt I required no defense since there was no basis for this separation. The judge read the papers.

Judge: "Mr. Mink, do you understand the charges?"

J.M.: "Yes, your Honor. I had them translated into English."

Judge: "Your wife wants you to vacate your *jointly*-owned apartment."

Judge, to Aviva: "Where are you now residing?"

Aviva: "In my Tel Aviv former home."

Judge: "Where would you suggest Mr. Mink should move to?"

Aviva: "Let him go back to the Tel Aviv Hilton *where I found him!*"

Judge: "I'm putting off my decision for a month. I strongly suggest at your next appearance, Mr. Mink, you retain the services of an attorney. These are serious charges. For the time being, you may remain in the apartment."

Aviva: "Your Honor, what shall I live on; he destroyed my legal practice?"

Judge: "You do have a home, a car and a practice. Case adjourned."

Finally a Stroke of Luck

One of the lawyers I was referred to inquired: "Are you married to the former Aviva Ranani? I suggest you employ the services of the lawyer who sent her ex-husband to jail in Switzerland!" (He had been extradited to face fraud charges in a notorious case.) This was none other than the right-wing activist and former Member of Knesset, Elyakim HaEtzni. HaEtzni, at this point had moved to Kiryat Arba, together with his wife and five children. He now occupied a sixty square meter apartment, after leaving his comfortable home in Ramat Gan, as an act of national/Zionist idealism. On contacting HaEtzni by phone in Kiryat Arba, I offered him a brief sketch of my tzuris (problems).

HaEtzni: "Mr. Mink, you have fallen into the hands of one of the most vicious and scandalous women I ever encountered." (Based on his work and intelligence from the case against Dov, her former husband.)

The Court Scene: Next Month

HaEtzni had acquired an associate for court appearances in Tel Aviv, Attorney Mati Sela. I had already driven to Kiryat Arba several times to plan my defense, and became friendly with the HaEtzni clan. When the court date arrived, I appeared with attorney Sela, and witnessed an unbelievable sight: Aviva came to court in an indescribable condition, wearing ill-fitting clothes (rags), perhaps from her teenage days. She was totally disheveled and bedraggled; a complete Purim stage costume.

Judge: "Mr. Sela, as the lawyer for Mr. Mink, how do you plead?"

Sela: "We refute all charges and claim this was a deception from day one, to separate a new American oleh from his possessions."

Judge: "Attorney Israeli, what is your position?"

Israeli: "You can see my client is in a pitiful situation. There is no income; this man has destroyed her practice. (That statement again!) You can read statements in his own writing to that effect. How shall Aviva survive until the court settles this case?"

I noticed, despite the costume of rags, Aviva had forgotten to take off the very expensive engagement ring. I brought this to the attention of my attorney.

Sela: "Your Honor, if she is so destitute she can sell the auto Mr. Mink gave her and the expensive engagement ring on her finger."

Aviva quickly removed the ring, but it was too late; the judge had also seen this action.

The Judge's Decision

The judge awarded me residence in my apartment. Noting what clearly was her deception, he awarded Aviva a minimal allowance (over her objections that I was an American millionaire) of perhaps $200 a month. And he strongly advised both attorneys that this matter should be resolved out of court. Aviva and her attorney stormed out of court irate. For once I had won the day. But an entire major episode lay ahead.

The Hollywood Stuntman

In the event that a studio decide to produce a movie of my life story (I'm joking), they'll need Kevin Costner or Harrison Ford to play this next scene. *Every word* is as close as possible to the truth.

Within a week of the court decision, on the morning of April 13, 1977, as I was leaving Barclay's Discount Bank on Allenby and Rothschild Street, in Tel Aviv, unbelievably I saw Aviva in my former used Ford car. She was pulling out of a parking lot across from the bank. I ran over (briefcase in hand) to speak to her about reconciliation. Neither she nor her lawyer would talk to us at this point.

When she spotted me, she rolled up the windows and locked the doors. I ran in front of the car to cause her to stop. She kept driving forward. I was driven backward at an increasing speed, in fear of being run over. I jumped on the hood of the car, spread-eagled. Aviva continued to drive, faster now. As we drove up the street, people were gawking at this surrealistic sight. I could see through the windshield that Aviva was also scared and irrational. Holding onto my briefcase with one hand and the windshield wiper apparatus with the other, I really thought this was my final day in this world. At this point, I received a bracha (blessing). We had traveled an entire city block with me on the hood. Remember, this was downtown Tel Aviv. When she reached the cross street, she slammed on the brakes. Via inertia, I flew off the hood, feet first, and fell sprawling on the ground, miraculously only tearing my clothes, plus some scratches, but not seriously hurt. The action continued. As I'm lying on the ground, dazed, Aviva makes a left turn to escape the scene. An English-speaking scooter driver stops: "I saw everything; get on the back: let's follow her till we find a policeman."

We began to chase Aviva's car, swerving in and out of traffic. She made another left, now heading back again toward Allenby. When she came to the light, thinking she had gotten away, she suddenly saw in her rearview mirror the Vespa driver with Jerry Mink in the back, in pursuit. She panicked, jumped the red light across Allenby, and was slammed into full force by a Dan passenger bus. Hard to believe, but she was unhurt. The car, however, was nearly totaled (though eventually repaired). The Vespa driver then asked me, "Who is that madwoman?" I answered, "My wife." On hearing this, he said he didn't want anything to do with a shalom bait (peace in the home) problem and drove off. I did write down his license plate number.

Interestingly, at a subsequent meeting with Aviva, she said, "You didn't even wait to see how badly I was hurt and help me out of my car." This is the real definition of *chutzpah*! I went to attorney Sela's office, and we filed a police report on this hit-and-run accident.

A Second Stroke of Luck

Following the judge's recommendation, we attempted to find a common ground to settle our divorce. Aviva and her attorney were adamant and greedy. Within a month, I went back to the States and invited a former girlfriend, Lynette, to join me in Israel. A few days after her arrival, while I was at work, Aviva and a city inspector entered the apartment to take an inventory for her lawsuit, as to what my possessions and apartment were worth. Finding my friend there, Aviva demanded that Lynette leave immediately, on moral grounds; I was living with another woman while we were technically still married.

Out of nowhere, Dov Ranani's brother, Shimon, called. He had learned that Aviva was suing me for divorce. He suggested we meet ASAP. He had some startling information to supply to me. A duplicate of a signed and notarized document is in my possession.

The Real Story of Aviva's First Marriage

Dov's younger married brother, Shimon, a business consultant, shocked me with his revelations.

1. Dov was a successful businessman when he met Aviva. Aviva came from a pathetically poor household. Her father had died much earlier by committing suicide.
2. When they considered marriage, like Jerry Mink, he had to clothe her; she had nothing to wear.
3. After marriage, Aviva continued her studies towards a law degree.
4. She pressed him to buy an apartment for the two of them.
5. Some years later, Aviva conceived Pia, and now demanded that they build a grand villa, well beyond their means, in an elegant area, Kfar Shemaryahu.
6. Short of cash, he inveigled some Swiss investors to enter his building material business, but instead used the money to build his villa.
7. He became suspicious of her fidelity after an incident in a parked car on the beach, reported by the police.
8. He retained a private detective, and together they caught her with another lawyer in a compromising situation at his office one evening.
9. After he was jailed in Switzerland, Aviva sold the incomplete house to pay off the debtors and get him released. Soon after, he sued for divorce on infidelity charges.

Shimon Ranani handed me affidavits validating this information. Now, suddenly, we had ammunition to fight with: first the hit-and-run affair, a subject of police record, and now a clear challenge to her fraudulent background. Please remember, her demands to meet my two ex-wives and check my history in America before she would approve the shidduch. Shimon Ranani really had a vengeful hate towards Aviva. We finally got Aviva and her attorney to sit down and negotiate a settlement. I was adamant against giving her any financial settlement. Attorney Sela: "Remember your goal; you want an end to this marriage, with a civil divorce and a get. Only Aviva can expedite this." Me: "But what about the hit-and-run and the deception?"

Sela: "OK. We bring civil and criminal charges. Suppose we win. Aviva sits in jail. The problem is when she gets out, she still owns half of your apartment. And you are still married without a divorce. And the fight goes on for years."

The Final Act

After several meetings, a financial arrangement was agreed to by both parties:
1. I would have to buy back "her" half of the apartment.
2. Compensating Aviva for "destroying her practice". (That expression again.)

After all the papers were drawn I had to come up with the cash, $50,000. I found a buyer for the apartment, a dentist from Edmonton, Canada, Dr. Eli Adler (subject of another chapter). As we sat down for the signing, I was totally consumed with anger and blurted out, "Don't think you're going to get away with this. I'll pursue and haunt you the rest of your life, just like Shimon Ranani." At this, Aviva leapt to her feet and shouted to her attorney, Israeli, "We're not signing!" and left the office.

My Attorney Sela was beside himself.

Sela: "You idiot, couldn't you keep your mouth shut for one more minute? She already had the pen in hand."

Well, there was no signing that day. Sela arranged another meeting, lawyers only. Aviva now demanded a document that I would not go near her or any member of her family; I would not contact them or threaten her again. If I did, there was a significant monetary penalty, perhaps $10,000. The final signing was done between lawyers. I think it was for the best, just a bad dream. Best in this case forgotten and erased with a check. As Yogi Berra, the ex-ballplayer and originator of "new expressions" said, "It was deja vu all over again!"

Just as Pauline, Papa's ex did, Aviva drove off with my car and a sizable check. I never contacted her, due to the threat of a lawsuit and significant penalty. For perhaps ten years I did not see her. Then, one day we literally bumped into each other in a Jerusalem court building. She didn't recognize me at first. Then, on recognition, she looked at me and said, "Oh, it's you." I suppose that was her identification code for another victim.

SELLING THE RAMAT AVIV APARTMENT

The local real estate market in 76/77 was extremely depressed, which explains how I bought the apartment originally for $155,000. I had invested an additional $25-30,000 for repairs, appliances, etc. The fact was, I needed cash, first to repay a Barclay's Bank loan after closing shop, and second, to ransom myself from Aviva Ranani's clutches. I established a non-negotiable price of $200,000 with a Tel Aviv real estate agent, a former American, giving him an exclusive agency. The combination of location, Neve Avivim, a 280 meter, twelfth floor penthouse, and the apartment being a twin (even till today) of one owned by Shimon Peres in the next building, brought crowds of lookers – not buyers – to my home each weekend. Acting to eliminate the schnorers, I told the agent that, henceforth, anyone wishing to see this showplace would have to pay $75. Shocked, the agent responded, "I've never heard of anything like this before." I told him, "*Now* you've heard everything."

Within a week, the agent called again.

Agent: "Mr. Mink, I have a serious buyer from Canada. Can they come up to inspect it?"

J.M.: "Sure, for $75."

Agent: "I give you my word of honor, this will be the absolutely final freebie."

Relenting somewhat, I said O.K., this is the last. That afternoon, Dr. Eli Adler and his wife, Phyllis, arrived.

Dr. Adler: "I had to see this place, just to meet the person with such chutzpah to charge $75 for a look-see."

They checked out the apartment quickly. Eli was a dentist in Edmonton, Alberta, and for years had been actively involved as a real estate investor. They were serious.

Dr. Adler: "Is this price negotiable?"

J.M.: "No, but we can negotiate over the payment terms."

We shook hands on a deal in five minutes. At last I was doing business with another North American Jew. What a pleasure! I later took a side trip to Edmonton to evaluate Adler's real estate holdings. They were really most impressive, with a book value in excess of $20,000,000. Within a few years, prior to his final payment, the real estate market in Western Canada collapsed. His highly leveraged properties were foreclosed by the banks. Dr. Adler repaid me every last dollar. In this case, my judgment was correct. Dr. Adler also finally sold this "bad luck" apartment to meet his debts, as he was now also under financial pressure. As I've seen many times in business, timing is of the essence, and in life over all.

Remarkably, within the last year, I read an ad in the newspaper; the apartment was again up for sale, this time for $985,000. Which proves that all the dollar figures I quoted have to be multiplied by four or five, in today's terms.

CLOSING UP SHOP AT ISRAELI RECYCLING COMPANY (HIL)[1]

From a distant perspective it might sound as though I just surrendered. Don't you believe that. My original plan was (since I was at the port in Ashdod) to export scrap steel to Italy or Spain.

My Discoveries:

1. When Koor, a Histradrut division, built the steel refinery in Acco, north of Haifa, the Labor government had given them an exclusive to purchase all the scrap steel generated in the country at *their* price. Plus, you needed their okay before you could export a single pound.

   So in effect, they could buy at their own price. For someone who cut his teeth in a capitalist environment, this was madness. Plus, the established price was the same for a dealer with one ton or 1,000 tons. The only differential was the distance you traveled to get to Acco.

2. The scrap purchasing division of Kiriat Pladot (Steel City) was a competitor having processing plants of its own.

3. The price they paid was *not* based on a world market price structure but in reverse. It was established to ensure Kiriat Pladot made a profit.

   So, in effect, if the cost of producing and selling was $100 a ton and their costs rose, they reduced the scrap buying price, regardless of world

---

1. Hevra Israel Le Michzur.

economic factors. It was pure socialism: never cut internal and labor costs.

4. While traveling, I saw thousands of automobile hulks abandoned which could be collected and turned into salvage. The Ministry of Transportation would not allow this without giving its permission for each abandoned wreck separately.

5. Trying to get export business for non-ferrous metal was also a bureaucratic morass.

6. Inflation ranged at the 40% level. In the USA, when I left it stood at 5%.

7. Interest rates for borrowed money were legal usury.

8. When you sold material to Kiriat Pladot, they decided what the terms of payment were (often 90-120 days, in effect reducing your profit by 15%).

9. Labor laws, Histadrut holidays, absenteeism, miluim (reserve military duty), periodic strikes, all maddening and destructive.

The Final Crusher

In Brescia, Italy, I had found a consumer, Capra Metal Refinery, for the aluminum scrap we collected. It was one small profitable area. They paid 100% against export documents. The two brothers were gentlemen. We had shipped several containers and were not paid. I called them many times. They claimed they paid. I flew to Brescia to straighten out matters and discovered my partner, Moshe Golan, had instructed them that the material shipped was Golan's, not IRC; we were merely his shipping agents. I flew back the next day, called Golan and told him I wanted him to repay me at once. I was totally out of control. I drove to his office in Tel Aviv (he said he would wait for me to make an accounting). Needless to say, on arrival he was out. I went berserk and overturned his desk. He filed criminal charges against me with the police. The next morning – knowing he left his home on Achad Ha'am Street in Tel Aviv at 6:00 a.m. – I was there, waiting by his car, at 5:30 a.m. When he came down, I told him, "This is the last day of our business relationship, or the next day one of us would be dead. You are a thief. Your ex-partner, Chaim, was correct. I have no one but myself to blame."

That evening we called in one of *his friends* to arbitrate and we settled our affairs. We were still partners in the Ashdod facility; I sold my 50% to one of his friends at a fraction of my cost. I sold off all the equipment and closed the operation. I became the living example of the adage: *If you want to make a small fortune in Israel, bring a big fortune.*

P.S. Eventually I discovered that my wife Aviva, whom I was in the midst of divorcing, was exchanging information with Moshe Golan.

Now you can see why I ran away into the desert to Yamit.

ONLY IN ISRAEL
#4

"Go away; don't bother us"

Several years ago the Ha'aretz newspaper carried a story of an American immigrant who had spotted a business opportunity in Israel. David Premovitz, who arrived in 1983, realized that in the multitude of old cars abandoned on roadsides there lay considerable scrap metal value. A repeat of the Y. Mink story.

Early in 1986 he came up with the idea of setting up a modern compression and extraction plant. Some parts could be used in steel production in Israel, others could be exported. The environment could benefit, too, since the wrecked cars, both an eyesore and an environmental hazard, would be promptly removed. It was a particularly attractive idea.

The inter-ministerial committee on recycling suggested giving the plant "approved enterprise" status; the environmental protection people were in favor and even suggested a site for the plant; and the Bank for Industrial Development supported the project.

Then, sadly, Premovitz ran into the inevitable bureaucratic runaround. The proposed site was vetoed by the IDF on the ground that it was an army firing zone. The inter-ministerial coordinating committee decided that the whole issue of scrap-collection had to be referred to regional councils. The Ministry of Industry and Trade decided that the plant's entire product would have to go strictly to local steel producers and not be exported. And so it continued. Once one obstacle was cleared, two new ones materialized. In the end, Premovitz gave up.

Amos Rubin, former economic adviser to the prime minister, put it frankly, "I am ashamed of the way Premovitz and his group were treated... This is an example of the inconsistency of the government's declared policy of encouraging investors."

Indeed, the government misses no opportunity to make loud noises about its commitment to attracting investment. It stresses the need to create jobs and increase exports. It offers a substantial package of inducements to putative investors.

But it completely, utterly, totally misses the point. Israel has a growing population, good climate, an advantageous location, a skilled workforce and high consumption levels. Political instability, often cited as a deterrent to investment, is no more of a risk than in Eastern Europe, which has seen a massive influx of investors since the fall of the Berlin Wall, or in Northern Ireland.

Foreign, and for that matter local, investors do not want "inducements." They want a level playing field, quick decisions and little, if any, bureaucracy. They do not want ignorant, unhelpful clerks who find absurd reasons to kill viable projects, or officials who worry more about their turf than the good of the country. If the government wants to attract investment to create jobs and stimulate growth, it had better start cutting red tape in a big way; and get the bureaucrats to learn to say "yes" nicely, quickly and often, much more often. And it had better do so soon.

YECHEZKEL THE MOVIE MOGUL
or
HOW SEVEN BEGGARS (ALMOST) BECAME EIGHT

It's a story I've told many times, of my first meeting with Gedalia (Glen) Gurfein, now Rabbi Gedalia. Arthur Gurfein, his father, and I had been members of the Shelter Rock Tennis Club on Long Island in the 1970's. We had rarely spoken, until one afternoon Arthur approached me in the locker room at the club. "Jerry, I hear you are doing some business in Israel and travelling there regularly." Still quoting Arthur Gurfein, the attorney: "My son was on his way to the Far East to investigate *other* far-out religions. On the way he stopped off in Israel for a look-see, and some group or cult seems to have entrapped him in Jerusalem. Next time you are there do me a favor and see what happened to Glen." He gave me his address and particulars and told me to remind Glen he had to return to Syracuse Unversity to continue his studies in the fall.

The saga expands; on my next trip, in 1974, I did find Gedalia. The cult that had ensnared him was the yeshiva, Ohr Sameach, and the group was the ba'al teshuva movement. In a memorable hour spent together, I learned Gedalia's story of a zero religious background and meeting two young men at the Wall who invited him to the yeshiva for one evening of listening and learning. Now, six months later, he was the epitome of a turned-on, born-again Jew. At that point I also met the Rosh Yeshiva, Rav Nota Schiller, who has remained my friend for the past twenty plus years.

In a memorable scene on my return to the tennis club, the father, Arthur, approached me anxiously. "Well, did you find my *lost* son?"

I replied, "Arthur, *you're lost*. Gedalia has found his place in the world." I'm still good friends with both of them.

Gedalia and I have climbed the path of return to religion, living through some happy events and our five marriages during our relationship, and numerous other experiences. (Detailed in other chapters.) However, this story is about Yechezkel and Gedalia's efforts to become major movie producers (moguls).

When my friend Gedalia gets an idea, it possesses him, and his enthusiasm stimulates all those around him. I've witnessed many such eruptions. Following his first divorce, from Shoshana, Gedalia and another yeshiva student, David Lenik, conceived the idea of employing the classic Chassidic tale of the Torah giant, Reb Nachman of Breslov, and bring it forward two centuries to create a full-length film. The fable is called *The Seven Beggars*, and I nearly became the eighth through my connection with this project.

On several previous occasions, Gedalia had become enthralled with ideas, but I had remained uninvolved. This one, with the excitement of a movie to be produced here in Israel, with the encouragement and assistance of the government's Division of the Arts, was all too tempting. I also caught the virus. Something I've learned over the years; everyone enjoys encouraging an interesting project until it becomes "tachliss time" (putting up the cash). It began with Gedalia and David writing a simple outline of a script and production. Whoever read it, loved it. Someone had to support the artists; meet Mr. Yechezkel. After much professional encouragement, a full-length script was created, thanks to Mr. Y's financial support. Then a trip to England and New York for collaboration and encouragement, plus lining up various artists and actors, thanks to Mr. Y.

Next, a first rewrite here in Israel, after significant encouragement by people on the sidelines, thanks to Mr. Y's support.

Now we were equipped with professional rewrite #2, plus added expenses, legal and secretarial, etc., thanks to Mr. Y's support.

The challengers to the world of MGM and 20th Century Fox decided at a board meeting (of this brains trust) that the place to present our potential Oscar-winning epic was Hollywood. Cost of travelling and six months maintenance, and contacting the powers that be (many were again encouraging), thanks to Mr. Y.

Hence the return to Jerusalem for another rewrite.

Mr. Y soon discovered that the path up the aisle to receive the coveted Oscar is strewn with many disappointments.

The final scene of our movie careers finds the gullible Mr. Y disillusioned and tired of writing checks. Gedalia Gurfein returned to his yeshiva studies and public relations work, remarried and divorced again. David Lenik went back to the States and now resides in New Jersey as a businessman. And Mr. Y's bank account shows a significant debit.

P.S. The script is in my home, on the spot where I planned to place the Oscar.

ONLY IN ISRAEL
#5

This brief missa (story) was related by Yaacov Kirschen, the cartoonist known for his "Dry Bones" strip, at a seminar given at AACI (Association of American and Canadians in Israel). Yaacov had made aliyah around 1970 and was deposited at an absorption center (mercaz klita) in Beer Sheva. Noticing he needed repairs on the soles of his shoes, Mr. K. inquired where this could be accomplished. He was directed to a shop in town: "You'll see a sign outside, 'sandlar' (shoe repairman)." With considerable difficulty, he located the sign and shop. It was a cellar level establishment: dark, dank and depressing.

On entering, Yaacov beheld this odd sight: on one side was the repairman, his work table and tools, plus piles of shoes in various stages of repair. On the opposite wall sat three men and a woman on a long crude bench. All were solemn-looking and absolutely silent. Possessing minimum Hebrew, Kirschen pointed to his damaged shoes. The cobbler, in a combination of Hebrew and sign language, asked to examine the impairment. Yaacov, standing on one leg, removed the shoe and handed it over. The craftsman examined it and in an amazing two-second motion, operating with a giant plier, tore off the entire sole. He then directed Mr. K. to the bench. The four occupants in unison moved over to give Yaacov room to sit and then began to converse in a monotone of whispered conversation. Strangely, when the next client arrived half an hour later, Mr. K. joined in this monastic ritual and watched the assault. He was now becoming an Israeli.

YAMIT
(LITTLE SEA)

The IRC disaster and Aviva ripoff were behind me. I had sold the apartment in Neve Avivim. Now arose the question, what to do with the rest of my life span and then, where to live.

With my new companion, Lynette, I decided to travel and investigate various areas of Israel. Initially I went north to Kiryat Shmona and Metulla, then south to Kibbutz Sde Boker in the Negev, where Ben Gurion then resided. As a matter of fact, I inquired as to the possibility of living there. They intended to develop a tourist facility; I felt I was ideally suited to organize and manage it, but on further investigation the kibbutz directorate decided I was too old at 50 to become a kibbutz volunteer or member. I had read of a new development in the Northern Sinai, encouraged and subsidized by the then Labor government. Its purpose was to expand the national borders and move the population down south, away from the narrow central strip. We stayed over at Beer Sheva and in the morning drove southwest to Yamit.

On approaching the town, one came upon a tall steel monument, perhaps six stories in height dedicated to the soldiers who fell conquering and holding on to the Sinai. Then the beautifully planned town, still under construction, with a small shopping mall, and the one kilometer walk to a clear, white sand beach with palm trees down to within 300 meters of the blue Mediterranean. A picture postcard setting. I inquired at once about the possibility to settle there. As usual there were bureaucrats, but I was given a lawyer's number in Tel Aviv to contact, Yehoshua Bar-El.

Yes, I could buy a villa for about $20,000. 50 square meters, 3 rooms, kitchen, and bathroom. All concrete and reinforced steel prefab construction. Since many of the residents were from a chug (group put together in the States, and transferred and subsidized for the early period), I had to sign an affidavit that I was self-supporting and would not ask for financial assistance. I had sold most of my furniture to the Adlers with the apartment, so I shipped some basics down from Tel Aviv. It was a dream setting. Lynette soon found a salaried position teaching English to the officers at a local army base. That had been her profession – English high school teacher.

Life seemed to have reached a measure of peace and continuity, when suddenly, out of nowhere, the Camp David accord (after Sadat's Israel visit) became a reality and I was back in the turmoil of picking up and moving again. There was a significant backlash from the local population. Some had moved from the States. Also, many Israelis had sold their homes up North. But, Jerry

Author in Yamit, 1979. After three divorces I was down to driving a bike

CHARLES JERRY MINK   צ'רלס ג'רי מינק
456   456
YAMIT, ISRAEL   ימית, ישראל

Oct. 4, 1978

Dear Rabbi,

I read your cautiously phased Prayers for peace and hope
for the new year 5739 in the Jerusalem Post Sept. 29, 1978.

What it failed to say (and what I was earnestly looking for),
is when you will start to lead your flocks back to our land.

As a new Olah and a person who is being resettled because
of the lack of Jews in our area (as I see it), I wonder
how you can approach the New Year and say to your flock,

 sound the great shofar for our freedom, raide the signal
to bring our exiles together; draw our scattered people
together from the nations; assemble our dispersed from
the uttermost parts of the earth. Bring us to Zion the city
singing, to Jerusalem thy santuary --- etc.
(the Prayer said before sounding the Shofar.)

What signal are you looking for?

What message do you expect to receive to start you and your
flock on their return?

Who but yourself can lead the disintegarating House of Israel
in the dispora, which is assimilating before your eyes?

If not now When?   If not through your leadership by whose?

                              Respectfully yours,

Mink, a newcomer to the country was not of a mind to oppose the decision of his newly adopted country and right-wing Begin government.

In truth, most of the opposition petered out when the government – with the financial backing of the United States – paid the population (for once) fairly. Lynette and I realized we also had no future together; no sense in unearthing this trauma. (She passed away of natural causes – lung cancer I'm sure – about 10 years later. She was a heavy smoker, our main area of discord.)

A Memorable Yamit Incident

While living in Yamit, I had begun considering becoming more observant. I had gravitated toward the 10-15 Shomer Shabbos Ashkenazi families and began a practice of going to synagogue on Shabbos.

The community was built on a master plan of a series of cul-de-sacs. Each had the wooden framework for a succa in its center. One of my observant neighbors suggested (as Succot approached) that we go into the "Sinai Desert" and cut down some S'chach (palm fronds) to cover the frame. Taking an ax, I was out in the midbar[1] when suddenly it dawned on me that I was performing a task performed a 100 generations before by Moshe Rabeinu and the people of the Exodus!

I'll close the Yamit chapter with another unforgettable saga in my life.

I continued to subscribe to the Jerusalem Post in Yamit. On September 29, 1978, a full page ad taken by 170 rabbis and congregations in the United States, congratulating the State of Israel for consummating the Camp David Agreement and its decision to vacate and return the Sinai to Egypt. On impulse again, I wrote a letter, addressed it to the approximately 100 rabbis who had supplied a mailing address in the ad. (The letter is on the previous page.) Surprisingly, I received about 20 responses, many congratulating me on my initiative and all in agreement: We should never have given up Yamit! But in reality it was all futile. The Yamit infrastructure, meant for 25,000 people, was occupied by 1,000-1,200 individuals. They were easily encouraged to move out by generous "payoffs," called pitsuim.

---

1. midbar – desert.

One final episode: Six months later I visited the States and was a Shabbos guest of Rabbi Meyer Fendel, referred to several times earlier. We davened that Shabbos at the same West Hempstead, Long Island, New York shul of the previously mentioned Dr. Schnall. The rabbi officiating was Sholem Gold. When I was introduced to the congregation by Rabbi Fendel, Rabbi Gold approached.

Rabbi Gold: "Are you the Charles J. Mink who wrote me from Yamit several months ago?"

Y.M.: "Yes, Rabbi, I wrote about 100 letters."

Rabbi Gold: "Mr. Mink, I received your letter and left it on my desk. I couldn't decide whether to throw it away or put it in my file. If you come to my study, you'll find it sitting there. It seemed to strike a chord in me."

Rabbi Sholem and Baila Gold made aliyah about five years later with Rabbi Meyer Fendel. Both families now reside in the Har Nof area of Jerusalem. Rabbi Gold had become a powerful, militant leader and teacher of religious, right-wing positions and has an active congregation of former American olim. We meet often at rallies and have remained good friends to this day. Rabbi Meyer Fendel is a co-principal at a girls' yeshiva, here in Jerusalem.

Postscript:

Following the Camp David agreement signed by Menachem Begin and Anwar Sadat on September 17, 1978:

There were high expectations of opening new vistas of trade between Israel and Egypt. This in reality over the past 20 years has proven exaggerated and wishful thinking. The basic antagonism of the Arab world toward Israel remains constant.

A few days after the historic signing, the director of Solel Boneh (the largest construction and engineering company in Israel and a division of the conglomerate Koor) was interviewed as to what were his expectations now that this new business opportunity had opened.

He replied: "Based on the work our forefathers did about 3,700 years ago on the pyramids, the Egyptians can feel confident that our workmanship and engineering will stand up to the test of time."

ONLY IN ISRAEL
#6

I had taken possession of my small cottage in Yamit and realized the bathroom shower was not enclosed. There was merely a metal extension pole for a curtain. To overcome the desert temperature we showered twice a day. Having my Western values still in place, I decided we needed an aluminum shower stall.

Amongst the ten or more shops in the Yamit Industrial Park was one emblazoned with the sign Aluminum Factory. I located the owner and described my need for an aluminum enclosure. Mr. Aluminum: "No problem – ein bayah." I escorted him to my home for measurements. After some price haggling we agreed on price, design and measurements. Within a reasonable period (by Israeli standards) Mr. Aluminum arrived one morning for installation. The work completed, he called me in for final approval.

JM: "It's very nice and fits well. Where is the glass to keep the water inside?"

Mr. Aluminum: "Adoni (sir), the sign on my shop says aluminum not glass. That's another trade."

I was dumbfounded and began to scream and jump up and down, to no avail.

The American freyer[1] paid the agreed price and then went to the shop named Glass and arranged for his services. We freyers never learn. But as the Israelis say, who asked you to come here?

Lesson #140 on living in Israel.

---

1. freyer – sucker.

YECHEZKEL MINK –
TENNIS CHAMPION OF YAMIT

Somewhere in the annals of tennis memorabilia, I dream there is a notation on the Open Tennis Championships played in the Israeli town of Yamit, in the northern Sinai, in 1979, and decisively won by your author.

The sponsorship for the event was the Yamit Sports Authority, headed by one Sima. The sports facility complex consisted of two tennis courts, basketball backboard and hoop, and a swimming pool under construction (and never completed).

The event was staged in an area that had fewer than 10 tennis racquets in the possession of its citizens and in a town of perhaps five potential players plus occasional touring visitors.

The finalists were:

Harry Wall – then a reporter covering the Sinai region and Yamit for the Jerusalem Post. Now director of the ADL (Anti-Defamation League) branch in Israel.

vs.

Jerry Mink – former scrap metal dealer. Former member of the Shelter Rock Tennis Club in Manhasset, LI, NY.

The spectators: Three local Beduins and the sports director, Sima, to give the event legitimacy. They were all confused, especially the Beduins, whose previous exposure to major league sport competition was non-existent. The climate and temperature of 105 degrees Fahrenheit in the shade were ideal for this Desert Classic.

After 90 minutes of grueling, vicious volleying and many questionable line calls, Sima awarded the former scrap dealer the first – and as it turned out, the last – Yamit Tennis Championship, sans trophy.

So a Mink finally entered the sports record books. The question is whether the Guinness Book of Records will accept my application for acknowledgment.

A VOLUNTEER
FOR THE JEWISH AGENCY (UJA)

It began in, of all places, the dining room of the UN in NYC.

A luncheon sponsored by the Israeli delegation at the U.N. was given for the honorees throughout the country at Israel Bond Dinners for the year 1976. I was presented to the assembly, for not only had I sponsored, and was the honoree of, a successful dinner at the Plaza Hotel in NYC, at which my friend Lt. Governor (at the time) Mario Cuomo was guest speaker, but I was also making aliyah in a few months, plus marrying an Israeli Sabra – wife #3, another major blunder (and chapter).

After the luncheon, a representative from the UJA approached with the suggestion that I should continue my efforts on behalf of the UJA even after aliyah. He handed me his card with the address of the Jewish Agency in Jerusalem on King George Street, and suggested I look up Mr. X, a director. In addition, I was given a one-year pass to play golf at Caesaria Country Club (never utilized).

Needless to say, after making aliyah, working to inject some life into my struggling recycling business, Israeli Recycling Company, getting married and divorced all within six months, then closing down the company and losing half a million of my personal dollars (subject of another sad chapter), moving to Yamit (also a chapter), etc., etc., volunteering to work for the Jewish Agency was a very low priority and definitely on the back burner.

After Camp David, and the decision to return Yamit and the Sinai to Egypt including with my small three-room all-concrete bungalow, I was now a free, unencumbered soul. But also one who was alone in a strange country, without language skills, significantly poorer and depressed, and asking myself, "What the heck have I done???"

Going over my papers while still in Yamit, I came across the UJA card, with a brief introduction to Mr. X. I decided to leave Yamit rather than fight the government decision. I made my application for pitsuim (a fund created to reimburse those forced to leave; for once, they were more than generous). I rented a small apartment in central Jerusalem with my things and with an unclear vision of my direction, and asking myself as I had often said to others: What are you going to do with the rest of your life?

At this point, my sister, Selma, tried to console me with the plea to come back to the States and become Jerry Mink again; all is forgiven! But instead, the impaired and damaged Yechezkel took the intro card, found the Jewish Agency Building on King George Street, Jerusalem, and was ushered into the offices of a director. And so began another chapter in my autobiography. The director, a fund-raising pro, was extremely cordial and receptive – why not? Here was a *volunteer* willing to assist. A former United States successful businessman, and most recently an evacuee from Yamit – great credentials.

At this point in time, Project Renewal was getting on stream, a plan which matched distressed Israeli communities with Jewish localities throughout the world. I was given a tour of several such areas in Israel: Jerusalem, Tel Aviv, Dimona, Holon, Haifa, etc., learned the sales pitch, and within a week I had a desk and telephone and became a fellow spokesman for Project Renewal in Israel.

In a short time I discovered that this was a specialty department handling the major donors, called in Las Vegas the "high rollers." This well-oiled division of the agency was a masterpiece in schnorring, an object lesson to behold.

The director had his private secretary and his executive assistant, Jackie (a relative and Shoah survivor, always prepared to retell his story of being imprisoned with Elie Wiesel). Mr. X had his personal car and chauffeur at his disposal year round, and seemingly unlimited expense accounts. When a group arrived in Israel, he set up residence in a King David Hotel suite to properly receive them. Plus, there were several trips a year to the States, always first class, to visit the home office in New York, and his children – who were yordim[1] in the USA.

A typical, oft repeated, scenario went as follows:

The aforementioned high rollers were urged to call before visiting the Holy Land, for special treatment and consideration. Mr. & Mrs. Y call from Cleveland. (This is prior to the computer age.) They are put on hold – there is another important call; a clerk who had an updated index card with all primary data on high rollers is alerted; she hurries to the director's office with card. The following conversation ensues:

Director: "George, how are you? How is Estelle (the wife)? Your married son, Jason, and his wife Suzy? Did your daughter Debbie graduate from Columbia Law School yet? (All carefully typed on index card.) Finally, when are you arriving? I hope you will visit us and allow us to offer you a car and chauffeur for..." $10,000 giver – one day. $20,000 – two days, etc., etc. If they were interested in Project Renewal, I would go along as the mouthpiece to the community that identified with their city (here, Cleveland). It was not that difficult an assignment: Chauffeur-driven, air conditioned car, lunches, nice, well-groomed, affluent people to converse with. But, the final curtain was the piece de resistance.

Director: "Well, George, I hope you and Estelle enjoyed our hospitality. We definitely enjoyed hosting you. It's a pity it was such a short visit this time. Please allow me to give you a personal goodbye gift. It's a book (usually a popular novel) which I just finished reading last night. It just happens to be here on my desk."

George: "Would you autograph it for us?"

Director: "Sure. It will be good for you to read on the return trip."

Unbeknownst to George, there were at least 40 more copies in his office closet. He naturally signs the book with flattering remarks. This chapter in my life lasted but a few months. I was overwhelmed by the mendacity and plain BS. Luckily, the Diaspora Yeshiva chapter came along.

---

1. yordim – literally, people going down.

THE DIASPORA YESHIVA

It has remained one of the major enigmas of my life's experiences – what is really going on, or what went on, at the Diaspora Yeshiva.

It began with a form of Divine Intervention (that phrase again). Seated one evening at the Plaza Hotel in Jerusalem, awaiting an appointment with someone who requested business advice (one of my grand deceptions), I found myself alongside Rabbi Mordechai Goldstein, his wife the Rebbetzin, and Shabatai Herman – a student at the yeshiva. The center of attention for the threesome was the quarry of every yeshiva, *"the Wealthy American Tourist"* (WAT). Unbeknownst to me, at that point in time, they had reached the climactic moment where the WAT was about to make some form of financial commitment – or at least exchange basic particulars. Suddenly the Rabbi exclaimed, "Who has a pen?" Yours truly possessed the implement. Again the Rabbi, "Do you have a piece of paper?" They were clearly not professionals (the Rabbi's strength would always be in teaching not fund-raising). I had this item also, whereupon the Rabbi finally took notice of me by saying, "Who are you?" I gave my secular name, Jerry Mink. The Rabbi, "What are you doing here?" I gave him a quick 20 word thumbnail sketch. His response: "Why not come up to the yeshiva to study?" The question was equal to NASA inviting me to become an astronaut. At this juncture, Shabatai had all the information or perhaps even a check from the WAT. He returned the pen with the remark, "How about coming to my wedding tomorrow night?" and handing me an invitation. As I mentioned in the previous chapter, I had become both jaded and disillusioned by my Jewish Agency activity, so with nothing to lose, the next morning I drove up to Har Tzion, the Old City location of the Diaspora Yeshiva. I had an extended conversation with Rabbi Goldstein and related my recent and former history. The Rabbi's decision – sit down and learn Torah, his standard remedy for all. He assigned me a tutor, who is now Rabbi Zahavi Green, and we delved into Pirkei Avot. I found it to be an astounding revelation of ideas, even as a Torah illiterate at that juncture. That evening I attended the Herman wedding – a human melee. It appeared Shabatai had been dispensing invitations by the hundreds for the past month. I made a prompt exit after congratulating all the principals, and within a week the Rabbi bestowed on me the title of Public Relations Director of the Diaspora Yeshiva (with some of my reservations intact). The next morning I again was at the Diaspora Yeshiva and came upon this scene. At the entrance to the yeshiva compound, which included study halls, offices, and living quarters for the single and married students, a crew from the Israel Electric Co. was ascending the steel pier on top of which lay the transmission box connecting the yeshiva to its electrical usage. The Rabbi and a number of students were assembled watching the workers. I inquired: "What's going on here?" Rabbi Goldstein answered that the electricity was being disconnected for non-payment.

"How much is owed?" I asked. Rabbi Goldstein, after a quick conversion calculation, said about $300. I pulled out my checkbook, made out a check payable to the Israel Electric Company. The workmen came down from the pole. Perhaps I had created a miracle: bringing light to where there was to be darkness!

The PR Investigation at the DY

I have always adhered to the Yiddish expression "Mi daf kukin foun avu the fess vaksin." (The loose translation is "first look from where the feet are coming.") I spent the next few weeks (with the Rabbi's permission) investigating – interviewing about fifteen new and veteran students and employees. The summation of my findings:

1. This was perhaps the oldest Ba'al Teshuva Yeshiva in Israel – in fact a pioneer.

2. There was a remarkable amount of talent and commitment; many looked at the Rosh Yeshiva as a father figure. Some had been Viet Nam War rejectionists and flower children of the 60s and 70s.
   Most were Americans and had arrived by chance. Like myself, most also arrived totally lacking Torah knowledge.
3. The Yeshiva had received gratis a very significant and valuable property, Har Tzion, shortly after the Six Day War. What was then an abandoned wasteland as a result of the Jordanian occupation, but what is now part of the Old City, plus many additional properties which have been occupied or purchased in and around the Old City. All this is under the control of the Diaspora Yeshiva and since it is operated as an oligarchy, basically the Rabbi's domain, and a Goldstein family monopoly.
4. The entire area of fund collection, distribution, and accounting was mysterious and secretive.
5. The loyalty and devotion of the talmidim and their wives to the Rosh Yeshiva was almost fanatical – even more than to a father figure.
6. The public image of the yeshiva ranged from 0 to -10.
7. I subsequently discovered that the Rabbi and my good friend Rabbi Meyer Fendel had been classmates at the Chofetz Chaim Yeshiva in NY. At my behest, R. Fendel came to the yeshiva to renew relations. Quoting Rabbi Fendel: "The primary concern of a yeshiva is to deal with public funds in a manner about which there should not be a shadow of a doubt."

As I delved deeper into the inner workings of the Diaspora Yeshiva, I discussed this with one of the older students whom I respected. He suggested that since the Rabbi was a man of letters, the best way to convey my information and questions to him was via a written document.

I thereupon drew up a multi-page fact and question sheet. I presented it to the Rosh Yeshiva. He read it carefully and responded, "I'll study this and give you a response shortly." That was fifteen years ago; I haven't received it to date.

How does a yeshiva get a negative image, since it is basically a seat of learning? I witnessed many events that created such impressions. A typical example follows: A certain American Jew had made a contribution to the yeshiva in memory of his brother who he thought had died in the Shoah. Years later he discovered that b"h[1] the brother had in fact survived. Being a simple Jew, he returned to the yeshiva and requested that the name be removed from a large memorial plaque of the names of the deceased. When the Rebbetzin heard his request, she demanded money for the erasure. The benefactor went berserk. There are volumes of such tales.

However, I did spend about two years at the yeshiva learning and helping with PR, where possible, and with some fund raising, but I eventually realized the PR work at Diaspora Yeshiva was fruitless and hopeless. I'm still friendly with many of the young men I met years ago, some of whom are still at the yeshiva after twenty or more years. Many have become rabbis themselves, some have left, most have married and become fathers and grandfathers; others have formed their own learning institutions.

There is an old Yiddish song I love singing. It translates to "when the rebbe dances all the students dance also." Since the Rabbi has fourteen children, his family, as well as his students' families, also grew. Most have now between 5-12 children. Needless to say, the facilities in the yeshiva compound were inadequate and property within the Old City skyrocketed in price. Fortunately, the '80s brought in a right-wing Likud government which created and subsidized many projects in Judea and Samaria. The Diaspora Yeshiva was allotted a settlement, subsequently named Metzad, where most of the families now reside and grow and grow and grow.

I feel it would be a disservice if I failed to credit the Diaspora Yeshiva for giving me new direction and assistance in beginning an Orthodox lifestyle, which I practice till today.

After marrying Hynda, I left the Diaspora Yeshiva and took a job at Bank Leumi, the subject of another chapter. Before leaving the yeshiva, I drew up a final fact and question sheet which the Rabbi read carefully, and placed it in the same right-hand top desk drawer with the remark, "I must evaluate this information and get back to you." Until this day, when we meet, usually at simchas, he recalls my reports with the remark, "Yechezkel, I still have your reports in my top righthand desk drawer." Years go by, the property is now

---

1. b"h – thanks to Hashem.

worth many millions of dollars, mailings for funds are systematically sent out by the office staff, with no accounting, except in Shamayim.[1] However, there are literally hundreds of Jewish children who would not be in this world, but for the Diaspora Yeshiva and Rabbi Goldstein's teaching.

---

1. shamayim – heaven.

ONLY IN ISRAEL
#7

Several years ago I committed what some might consider a questionable vehicular turn in mid-town Jerusalem. Who was waiting for me as I completed this maneuver? A policeman in civilian dress driving a civilian type car with red plates (a police official). He leaped out of his vehicle and began to berate me with an onslaught of gushing Hebrew which I could never decipher in a hundred years, and finished off with "lets see your papers." This much I understood. I replied in simple English trying to explain this questionable moving violation.

Police – (in Hebrew): "What, you don't speak Hebrew?

Me – (in English): "Not well enough to defend my supposed offense."

Policeman – (in Hebrew, perusing my documents): "What?! You have been in this country for 15 years and you still do not speak good Hebrew?"

Me – (in English): "Then I suppose you should give me 2 tickets – one for improper driving and another for language deficiency."

The policeman (trying to contain a smile) began to search in his car for something to record my "particulars" on. The only thing he came up with was a pizza cardboard square, well embossed with the remnants of grilled cheese from a once delicious slice.

He began recording my particulars, gingerly leaping over the encrusted cheese ridges. At this point I began to suspect that I would probably never hear about this confrontation again. And so it was...

ORIGINALLY APPEARED AS AN ITEM IN "YOUR JERUSALEM" 1995.

ADDRESS BY NY LIEUTENANT-GOVERNOR MARIO M. CUOMO

Before the Israel Bond Rally, Thursday, April 1, 1976
Plaza Hotel, New York City

I've known Jerry Mink for several years. I knew him even before he became sophisticated and grew a beard. I met him when I was a practicing attorney, and he was in business – Cousins Metals. I worked very hard for him. Frankly, I'm not sure Jerry appreciated those efforts as much as I thought he should. But then Jerry always had a reputation for making other people feel as though they owed him something. I can tell you that one of the reasons I was forced to give up the law practice and turn to politics to make a living was the size and infrequency of the fees I was able to extract from Jerry for services rendered.

Indeed, if I have as little success tonight getting you to buy bonds, as I had getting Jerry to pay his fees, I'll probably get an award from the PLO!

But I'm not here to tell you the *truth* about Jerry Mink. I'm here to say nice things about him. Shelly Gering said that before I became a politician I probably wouldn't have been able to disguise the truth so well as I can now.

I am here to join in a well deserved tribute to an extraordinary individual. A man who, having made his own way relatively early in his life, turned most of his energies to serving others. And particularly to serving Israel. I can recall a few years ago talking to Shelly Gering, his partner, about a matter of some concern to the business. And being told that Jerry had dropped everything to go to Israel because he felt he was needed more there.

Your program describes how he went to Israel to work in transportation and later, on a kibbutz, how he set up the Israeli Recycling Company and how in many other ways at considerable sacrifice to himself he has dedicated his energies to the advancement of a cause in which he – and all of us here this evening – believe deeply: the sustaining and enhancing of Israel.

I was pleased to come here tonight with my wife to join you in a tangible expression of our admiration for this man. I wish you, Jerry, and the sponsors of this lovely affair to know that you honored both my wife and me by permitting us to share in honoring you.

THE INTIFADA

The expression that I believe best expresses life in Israel is: "You may die of many things here, but never of boredom."

In the late 1980's, I met two former Kach activists; both had served time in administrative detention, a British Mandate law to put people on ice so the government authorities can continue to operate unimpaired and unopposed. They had both been jailed for supporting Rabbi Meir Kahane's positions. Both had families to support.

I had often toyed with the idea of starting a first-class limousine service for touring and airport pickup. Here were two capable young, bilingual former Americans. Ideal for the purpose. I sold them on the idea and formed a new corporation, "Three Americans." We purchased two used Volkswagon vans. The timing could not have been worse. The intifada had just burst out on the Israeli scene. The tourist business vanished. Then came the scud war with Iraq. We tried to convert the business to school children transport, industrial employee transfer. We bought additional larger vans, a bus. One of the original partners proved to be a non-starter. With Baruch ben Yosef and other employed drivers, we tried everything to reverse the losses. At the end of three years, I closed operations with a substantial loss and sold off the four vehicles. My record of Israeli business ventures was consistent and bad.

In between, after leaving Bank Leumi, I began another company, The American Way, for buying, renovating and reselling apartments around Jerusalem, with Neil Sher, a South African. That was moderately successful. However, the tax structure did not allow for quick turnover and short profit.

And at the start of the mass Russian aliyah of 600,000, the government provided them with mortgages. This drove the apartment market sky high – there were no metziahs (bargains) around.

An interesting incident happened to me during the intifada. A right-wing action to counter the Oslo Agreement planned to start shadow settlements next to existing ones. It demanded chutzpah and commitment, both of which I think I possessed.

Shawn Casper, a young attorney in his late 20's, Fred Moncharsh, a co-right-winger and former Kachnick in his early 40's, and I resolved to join the new shadow settlement movement and probably get arrested for defying the government directive against new settlements. It was a bitterly cold, wet winter evening. The three of us drove out to an area in Gush Etzion next to Moshav Ma'ale Amos. I had packed a handbag, assuming I'd be arrested. It seems the police and army authorities had been forewarned, and on our arrival they were waiting.

Only in Israel

They stopped our car. The officer in charge looked in and said, "This is not a night to camp out, especially for you grandpa (meaning yours truly). Chaverim (friends), go back home to your warm fires. Come back in the spring." And so we sheepishly turned around.

The period of intifada actions and counter actions had the country in constant turmoil. I took part in many demonstrations against the Rabin-Peres-Beilin troika. At times, hundreds of thousands took part. Mostly this was not publized by the leftist media. But eventually, these many actions and massive public demonstrations helped lead to a return to the nationalistic, right-wing government of Bibi Netanyahu.

ONLY IN ISRAEL
#8

Having finally terminated operations at the Israel Recycling Company (IRC), I was still half owner of a valuable industrial property in the Ashdod industrial park. My partner, M. Golan, had so abused my trust, I could no longer even face him. A mutual friend, D. Ostrofsky, approached me. I admired Ostrofsky. With a former kibbutznik partner, he was a hard-working and successful owner of a heavy construction equipment firm. Ostrofsky: "My good friend Jerry Mink! I know all about your problems with Moshe Golan. You do not understand the Israeli mentality. If you wish, I will buy your equity. I'll exchange my smaller migrash (plot of land) in the industrial area, plus cash, for your property to extricate you so you'll be finished with Golan forever." Not quite true. Just for the record, Golan eventually sued me for back rent on OUR property.

I quickly agreed. I had already sold my Ramat Aviv apartment and I now lived in Yamit. I wanted to forget the entire IRC disaster. Ostrofsky and I went to the lawyer where the deal was promptly finalized. Ostrofsky arrived at the bank the following day to transfer the "cash" to me. It consisted of: Israeli lira, USA dollars, British pounds, Belgian francs, French francs, and millions of Italian lira in various sums and denominations! If I hadn't seen it, I'd never have believed this balagan.[1] I brought the paper bag – yes, paper bag – filled with the money to my bank, where they confirmed the value was approximately the amount that was due.

---

1. balagan – mess.

Postscript. Now Mr. D. Ostrofsky was partners with the wily M. Golan. Several years later I ran into Ostrofsky. He told me this unbelievable story. He called for a meeting with his new property partner, M. Golan, to establish their relative positions in the company. Ostrofsky: "Let's go to a lawyer and write up a formal agreement."

Golan (the fox) took a paper napkin and wrote up the basic agreement.

Ostrofsky: "What are you doing?"

The Fox: "Writing up a preliminary agreement to take to the lawyer."

Ostrofsky: "You expect me to sign on this scrap of paper napkin?"

The Fox: "Why not? It's an agreement; we're friends."

P.S. The agreement never got past the paper napkin stage. Several months later, Golan arrived with another scrap dealer who purchased Ostrofsky's equity. The Fox used Ostrofsky to deal with me and get his hands on the property. When they presented the paper napkin to the lawyer, he also realized who the Fox was.

ANDERMAN TALES

Preface: I have always considered Buddy Ba one of the cleverest people I ever met and have urged him to write his own memoirs. Basil Anderman (alias Buddy Ba) and I have been friends, fellow boy scouts, neighborhood pals, and consistent critics of each other's life styles and directions for 60 years. Davka (in spite of this) we have maintained a strong bond. As Ba says, if we had lived in the same areas for the past 50 years the relationship would never have survived.

Background

Rabbi Dr. Anderman, his father, was my cheder teacher and bar mitzvah rabbi at the local Conservative Northside Hebrew Congregation, serving parts of Jackson Heights and Corona, Queens. (My mother, z"l, idealized Rabbi Anderman.) Rabbi Dr. Anderman was the recipient of a PhD in philosophy from the University of Vienna and had studied for the rabbinate to stay out of the Austrian Army in World War I.

This brilliant man became a casualty of history. In the 30's and 40's period of American Jewish experience, the majority of clergy were entrapped and assigned a low socio-economic status. Providing him with an income that was barely at subsistence level, the Jewish community (still affected by the Great Depression) felt a minimal responsibility for maintaining the shul and rabbi properly. As a consequence, his wife Anna, mother of their three sons, Basil, Armand and Alan, was forced to take a fulltime job, after years of barely surviving. She was employed as a clerk for a Western Union office in Grand Central Station in New York City. The three sons grew up untended, needy of affection and a normal home life.

A Historical Perspective

1. The financial and social power of the early Jewish arrivals to the United States was the German Jews, who arrived in the 19th century, with the residue of Reform Judaism in their luggage. They were disdainful of the Eastern European Jews who, they felt, lacked culture. This has been discussed in several books and studies.

2. The Jews of the mass exodus from Eastern Europe were associated with the Orthodox stream. Upon their arrival in New York, we are told, they figuratively, and in some cases literally, threw their tallis, tefillin and religious practice overboard in order to assume a fresh identity in the New World. They would not be impeded by Old World customs and tradition.

Basil's rise to social and financial success was definitely not from a level playing field. Rather, he first had to climb out of the pit of insecurity and poverty.

Always an above-average student, he applied first to the Merchant Marine Academy at Kings Point, Long Island, NY. He became a midshipman (primarily to escape home and get regular nutrition, and an education). He then applied for a NROTC (Naval Reserve Officers Training Corps) program in the U.S. Navy, which provided eligible young men with a four year university education in many of the best universities in the States. In exchange, the government demanded they accept a commission in the regular Navy and serve two years. At the University of Southern California, Ba became a campus activist, and resigned his commission. But he was allowed to finish school, which was what he actually wanted. He received a degree in behavioral science. On campus he met Evelyn, the chairperson of the debating team. They married after graduation. With the arrival of three daughters, the problem of supporting a family arose. Ba found an ad placed by IBM for a salesman with a background in engineering. He spent a day in the library cramming engineering basics and was hired.

The 1st Anderman Tale

It's inconceivable today that the product line of IBM in the late 1940's was office and workplace timeclocks and electric typewriters. Ba solicited this business with modest success. In despair one day in downtown Los Angeles, he gazed around and saw the massive clock on a bank building. The flash of genius: Why not have a giant digital clock on the bank? Ba made his way through a maze of managers and finally sold this concept to the president.

He returned to the home office with an agreement (unpriced). His office was ecstatic; what a breakthrough. It later dawned on the management that a giant digital clock would first have to be developed. After incurring some religious prejudice, normal in the period of the 40's and 50's, he moved on and began selling insurance, again at the bottom of the rung, door to door, based on telephone leads.

The 2nd Anderman Tale

One of his early insurance sales was to a Margolis family (not their real name) in Los Angeles. The clock moves forward 20 years and Ba is now in the *Anderman Company* offices in Century City, Los Angeles. Surprisingly, one day he was contacted by Mrs. Margolis.

Mrs. M: "Mr. Anderman, thanks to your insistence we purchased a life insurance policy for my husband, Benny, now deceased. I have just received the check for $25,000 and again request your advice. How should I invest this money to insure my son, Milton's, education?"

B.A.: "Put it in a time deposit (C.D.). If I find a better investment avenue, I'll call you."

Several weeks pass. Ba is contacted by a go-go stockbroker.

Broker: "Mr. Anderman, I have this venture capital stock situation that must skyrocket once it goes on the market. I'd like to see you buy some *now* at its opening price of 4. It definitely must jump to 5½ in a few days."

B.A.: "OK, buy me 5,000 shares." Suddenly, the spark of genius. "I'll call you back in a few minutes."

BA calls Mrs. Margolis, and explains the opportunity for a quick profit.

Mrs. M.: "Mr. Anderman, I'm in your hands. I know nothing about stocks, but with your OK, let's do it."

B.A. calls the broker. "Make that 7,500 shares."

With that he forgets the entire scenario.

Several days later, the invoice for the 7,500 shares arrived. BA called Mrs. M. to cover the purchase cost of the additional 2,500 shares.

BA: "Mrs. Margolis, please send me a check for $10,000 plus buying commission to cover the stock purchase."

Mrs. M.: "When will the stock be issued."

B.A.: "Probably this week."

Mrs. M.: "Do you want me to break the time deposit and pay the penalty for prior withdrawal? After all, *you* did suggest a time deposit."

B.A.: "OK, I'll advance the $10,000 and sell it ASAP. You're correct, why break the C.D."

Mrs. M.: "Thanks again, Mr. Anderman."

Several weeks pass. Ba has forgotten the matter. One morning, Mrs. Margolis is on the phone. "How is *my stock* doing?"

B.A.: "Hold the line, I'll check up." He called the stockbroker on a second line.

Stockbroker: "Yes, Mr. Anderman, the stock was issued. I didn't believe it, but it *did not* take off as expected."

B.A.: "Where is it now?"

Stockbroker, "Around 3½-3⅝, but holding steady."

Basil hangs up.

Mrs. M.: "Well, how are we doing?"

B.A.: "Truthfully, it did not sky-rocket as expected."

Mrs. M.: "I'll tell you the truth. *I really don't like playing the market.* Just sell my 2,500 shares and send me a check on the profits."

With no safety net in sight, Ba sent her a check for several hundred dollars *profit*.

Anderman Tales #3

By this junction, Ba has made a significant success as a private insurance agent. The same spark of genius had convinced him, why sell individual policies, e.g., Mrs. Margolis. Better to sell group health and life insurance plans to hundreds and then thousands. On visiting his Century City office in the 70's, I found it decorated with "million dollar salesman" framed certificates, plaques, awards, etc. My friend, Ba, had become a success story, perhaps a legend, and very wealthy as a consequence.

One of the insurance providers in London, England, chose to present him with an all-expenses paid grand trip and visit to their home offices as a gift. On arrival, Ba was presented to the chairman of the organization.

Chairman: "Mr. Anderman, we're pleased to welcome you to our home offices. As a gesture of recognition for the business you have supplied us, please join us at our club for a traditional luncheon given for special guests and friends."

At the club dining hall, Ba was seated at the guest of honor position at a large table. To open the luncheon, the chairman presented Ba formally to the assembled.

Chairman: "As our guest, it is traditonal that you choose the wine for this occasion."

Handed the extensive wine list, Ba realized he was in very, very deep waters. Addressing the chairman, Ba replied, "Sir, I'm the elder son of an American rabbi. The only wine I am familiar with is Manischewitz Concord Sabbath Wine. Since I do not see it on this list, I'm forced to pass the privilege back to you."

The chairman, obviously taken back: "Mr. Anderman, I personally am overwhelmed by your modesty and self-confidence. The wine choice was merely a gesture. Your stalwart character and honesty explain why you have become a success."

Today

At this point, Ba is divorced some 25 years, two of his three daughters are married and he is a proud grandfather. Ba resides in a lavish apartment in the Westwood area of Los Angeles. I'm pleased we have kept the lines open over all these years in spite of our very divergent life styles. Ba is now retired and has a rewarding relationship with a charming lady, Ita Adelstein.

Finale

An analogy Basil often quotes: "We all perform many demonstrative acts for our public, assuming our every action is being carefully observed, when suddenly the theater lights are turned on and we realize there is really no one out there."

THE CHOFETZ CHAIM
AND AUNT JEANETTE

In 1985 I arranged for a visit to Israel by my Aunt Jeanette, Mama's sister. At that point she was 73 years of age and widowed. As she was the last survivor of that entire generation of my blood-related aunts and uncles, I felt a need to expose her to my world, plus gain insight into some points of historical value in the family tree on the maternal side.

She told me many stories about my Zadah and mother's family which I recorded on tape. The most astounding is this:

At the close of WWI, as a result of the war, famine and general deterioration of the public health system, a deadly flu epidemic engulfed central Europe and particularly Poland, as first Germans, then Polish and Russian armies battled back and forth. Millions died. Jeanette remembered how week after week more desks were empty in her class as children fell victim to the epidemic.

Finally, Jeanette herself became infected and deathly ill. On learning that the Chofetz Chaim was visiting Bialystok, my Zadah Nahum Haim carried her to the yeshiva where the tzaddik was staying and asked for a blessing for his sick daughter, which she received. During the epidemic, her two brothers, Abraham and Elyakim, expired. Not only did Jeanette recover, she outlived all her siblings.

Jeanette passed on at the age of 85. Her final five years were spent, unfortunately, at an Alzheimer's institution, where she was supported by her nephews and nieces.

THE REMARKABLE
RABBI UZIEL MILOFSKY, Z"L

Those who are fortunate to be granted the opportunity to sit in the presence and absorb the learning and midos (values) of a great rabbinic scholar and teacher are blessed. Such was my good fortune via Rabbi Uziel Milofsky, z"l.

When you enter the ba'al teshuva world at 50+ years, there is endless ground to cover once you realize your deficiency, and precious little time to work on yourself. I suppose that's where the expression "a little knowledge is dangerous," came from. After leaving the Diaspora Yeshiva (as previously covered) my learning went into a hiatus. Following the Hynda divorce, I invited Chaim Tchaikofsky, my former teacher at the Diaspora Yeshiva, to provide me with private instruction for two years, and then I began a regular morning learning routine with Rabbi Jeremy Fenster, also of the Diaspora Yeshiva, who resided in the Old City.

At some point I learned of a teacher at Yeshiva Ohr Sameach, reported to be outstanding, Rabbi Uziel Milofsky. I began to attend his classes twice a day. if at all possible, to absorb like a sponge his vast reservoir of knowledge. Whether covering the Sefer HaChinuch, the review of the 613 Mitzvahs (a Jew's obligations), or the weekly Torah portion, his wealth of knowledge was enormous and his instruction penetrating.

Background

Rabbi Uziel was born in Uruguay, where his father held the position of Chief Rabbi of that country. He began his many years of learning to obtain ordination (smicha) at Ner Israel, in Baltimore, Maryland, and then at a yeshiva in Toronto, Canada. After serving in that community, this outstanding scholar was appointed Chief Rabbi of Mexico (Spanish being his mother tongue). In addition, his comprehension of English, Yiddish and, of course, Hebrew were all amazing.

Rejecting what was an esteemed position in the rabbinic hierarchy and a well-paid life-term chair, he chose to make aliyah with his wife, Chaya, and their five children. He settled in Jerusalem as teacher, lecturer, and guide for the talmidim at Ohr Sameach Yeshiva, involved in outreach programs. As his renown grew, the Reichman family of Montreal elected him to head an innovative program. Since the economy in Argentina had deteriorated in the late 1980's, they realized that for a minimal dollar investment – perhaps $50.00 a month per student – they could operate a full-time major Torah-learning institution in Buenos Aires and instruct thousands. Our Rabbi Milofsky was chosen to head this project. With disappointment we said goodbye to our teacher. In the final days prior to his departure, he suddenly became ill. I visited him at Shaarei Zedek Hospital. Our two families had become almost as one and exchanged visits or dinners with each other. His two younger children, a boy, Jonathan, and a daughter were very interested in BatSheva's (wife #5) botanical gardening work. After the stomach cancer operation, his strength deteriorated markedly. The Argentina proposal was cancelled and he gradually returned to teaching at Jerusalem's Ohr Sameach.

Transfer to Toronto

Two of the earliest benefactors of Yeshiva Ohr Sameach had been Mr. & Mrs. Joseph Tanenbaum of Toronto. Mr. Tanenbaum now called on the yeshiva to staff a giant synagogue and Talmud Torah he had established in Thornhill, Ontario, a suburb of Toronto. The Rabbi and his family were resettled in that community, and in 1992, on a trip to the United States, I took a side trip and visited the Rabbi for the final time.

Some months later, Rabbi Milofsky left this world. The entire yeshiva went into a Memorial Day schedule. Many tears and fond goodbyes were uttered to this scholar, teacher and role model. He was truly a giant among men.

RABBI MEIR KAHANE, Z"L

I first met the Rabbi in the late 1960's. He had been invited to my Conservative synagogue on Long Island, to debate, with an establishment person, his slogan "Every Jew needs a Twenty-two!"

I have always possessed an empathy for the underdog. The Rabbi was being assaulted on all sides for his aggressive stance, but he appeared more than capable to defend his position, obviously a veteran of many such skirmishes. After the meeting, I introduced myself and we exchanged a few words. I accepted some of his literature and placed my name on his mailing list. I soon began receiving invitations to JDL (Jewish Defense League) meetings and eventually, fund-raisers.

The Rabbi was outspoken and forthright. "The Jews in America are in mortal danger" from the extreme right wing, the Black Panthers, Ku Klux Klan, hostile Arabs, and other fascist, pseudo-Nazi groups. At one such meeting, Howard Ginsberg approached me. "You look like a man we should have in the Shtarkers." (The strong ones called on to defend Jews in the city ghettos under attack.) Howard was a giant man – 6'5" and 280 pounds at least. On impulse (again) I enlisted but soon forgot my new association.

One afternoon, while at work, I received a call at my office. "Jerry Mink, the Shtarkers organization calling; come ASAP to Brooklyn College. Our Jewish students are under attack." My reply: "Call the police. I'm busy making a living and let the students stand up for their rights. They are not feeble or incapable of defending themselves." With this, I resigned from the Shtarkers, and pursued other avenues to help our fellow Jews, and heard nothing thereafter.

Perhaps fifteen years had passed. I was now living in Jerusalem and began again to follow the fortunes of Rabbi Kahane, z"l. He was now making statements, staging demonstrations opposing the establishment and government policy in Israel. I started to attend meetings at his Ussishkin Street headquarters and became friendly with many of his followers in Israel. I again found Howard and Barbara Ginsburg; they had followed the Rabbi to Israel. I also deemed the rhetoric of standing up to the Arabs rational. The Rabbi felt his message could best be presented on the political front, as a member of the Knesset. He had organized a political party "Kach" (To Take) and ran initially in 1973. He was defeated badly in his appeal to North American olim. At some point, he was placed in jail, under administrative detention, a method of jailing a person to put him on ice and out of the public's awareness. In my opinion, while in jail he discovered that his message of forcefully confronting the Arabs was much better understood by that segment of the population who had lived under Arab repression, the Sephardim, formerly from North Africa. A high percentage of prisoners was from this group, and while incarcerated he concluded they were the address for his position, not the fragmented and liberal former North Americans. Rabbi Kahane finally won a seat in 1984. I attended the victory event with my daughter, Jackie, who was visiting at the time. I had campaigned and contributed to his campaign. Now, finally, the Rabbi had a platform, and he attacked all sides, urging for a country subject to Torah law and free of any Arab population. (One of his books, "They Must Go" deals with this subject.) This aggressive right-wing message was getting through, and as the next election approached, the consensus was that the Kach party would move from one Knesset seat to perhaps 5-7 (a significant faction).

The Establishment in Israel felt threatened. Here was a right-wing ideologue without political debts, only his principles. In what I consider the most vile, undemocratic procedure, Kach and the Rabbi were disenfranchised by the Supreme Court and not permitted to run in the elections. It was a horrible blow to those who had supported Rabbi Kahane and those who had sat in jail for months as Kach activists.

The anti-Zionist Arab Rights, Communist and assorted red flag waving left-wingers were allowed to run. But not this Israel-first, Torah law and lover of his fellow Jews advocate. This was a low watermark for Rabbi Kahane. He had lost his seat, and with it, his privileges. The Kach party had lost its automatic government funding, and several of his stalwarts, mainly from Kiryat Arba, outside Hebron, were again jailed for their ultra right-wing activities.

Rabbi Kahane continued his program via a new institution: *The Museum of the On-going Holocaust*, and was continually harassed by the government and left-wing elements.

The Rabbi gave several political seminars a week at the "Museum." Its walls were decorated with pictures and publications of anti-Semitic North American literature. On one particular evening, a cold rainy Wednesday night, I was the only one to attend his seminar. It was a bit embarrassing, sitting alone in the room. Eventually the Rabbi appeared. We sat down, one to one, and in his usual straightforward manner, he asked, "What would you like to talk about?" "Rabbi, I respect your ideology and commitment to our Jewish People. But how do you deal with the many lives and families that have been affected adversly and partially dismembered for following your ideology?"

The Rabbi replied: "I never sent anyone to a place or situation that I and my own children would not go. If they wind up in jail, we have also been there in defense of our cause, and for our love of my Jewish People."

That was the message he continued to pursue till the end of his life on December 5, 1990. He was gunned down by a fanatic Arab murderer at a New York City rally, exactly the people he warned would attack the American Jews. The killer was found innocent of murdering the Rabbi and wounding another person in his escape, in spite of being witnessed by a hall full of spectators. The self-hating Jewish attorney, William Kuntsler, used the ineffective, partial jury system to find this animal innocent (Shades of O.J. Simpson's – first trial). My daughter, Jackie, called me from the States in the middle of the night to deliver the news of his murder. She understood my admiration for this Jew who gave his life for our people. The killer was again indicted, and is now serving time for his participation in the World Trade Center bombing, where many more people were killed. So much for the American justice system.

I'm certain history will write a fitting epitaph for this heroic leader of the Jewish People, Rabbi Meir Kahane, z"l.

A RECOLLECTION OF MY FIRST ISRAELI EXPERIENCE

As I organize my thoughts and recycle events of twenty years ago, I am experiencing significant pain and discomfort. If I consider myself so smart, how did I allow myself to become so dumb? Another thought – the mind is a fantastic apparatus. It permits you to store away the painful incidents and place them out of view as in a closet, so that you can continue with your life. I suspect that countless thousands of institutionalized people lack that closet apparatus for confining distressful memories.

In passing, it should be noted that during the Ranani-Golan period I developed a condition in which my right eye would flutter uncontrollably. An M.D. told me it was a neurological reaction to inner trauma and pain. (A release.) As my friend, Mike Kramer of Jerusalem says, "There is no free lunch!" And as Frank Sinatra sings, "I did it my way."

Oy, it hurts.

ON BEING SINGLE
(SEVERAL TIMES)

As previously noted, I am a veteran survivor of five marriages. Naturally, between each, and prior to the first, I met many members of the fair sex. Several such affairs stand out. This book gives me license to record these for posterity. Please accept that *I DO NOT LIE*.

It is my observation, most single people prepare a tape reviewing their former life's activities. On request, the recording is activated and out pours a well-ordered version, which has been played over many times mentally, and then, verbally. Almost invariably, each event is orchestrated to insure it appears in the best possible light. Divorced former mates are usually despicable. Those that pass on prior to the surviving mate are "people we'll never be able to replace (find again)."

Episode #1

After separating from Bea, my second wife, I inquired of a divorced male neighbor, could he suggest someone for me to date. He provided the name and telephone number of a young, attractive Jewish widow in the area. I arranged a dinner meeting, which was laden with tales by the grieving widow about her tzaddik, Bill. Each successive meeting was a repeat performance; Bill this, and Bill that; what a wonderful mentsch. After the third or fourth such evening, Helen (not her real name) advised me that she would be out of the social scene for at least a month.

Helen: "I'm having my right forearm bone reset. It never healed properly after my accident several years ago."

Innocent Me: "A skiing injury?"

Helen: "No, it was broken when Bill threw a lamp at me and I put up my arm to deflect it!"

Episode #2

On a visit to the States, I was browsing through the New York Magazine personals – or shidduch ads. I find them clever and very well authored. One caught my eye:

DJW (Divorced Jewish woman); religiously committed; school-teacher; grown children; loves sports, Israel, etc.

I tore out the ad and weeks later, on my return to Israel, I sent an introductory letter to the P. O. Box at the magazine. Several weeks passed and I finally received a response. "I'm quite interested in your letter; let's correspond."

I wrote again and heard nothing for perhaps a month. One evening, I received a call: "We are the family of the woman you have contacted in New York. Since we are in Israel on a tour, please come by our hotel here in Jerusalem for coffee."

At the hotel lobby I met the brother, sister-in-law, sister, nieces, nephews, and assorted friends of my shidduch. I was being examined for further consideration. After coffee, the sister burst forth, "I'm certain I couldn't find a better shidduch for our Malka (not her real name)." Great. I passed the first hurdle. In short order the phone calls and letters accelerated significantly. Yes, it was all systems go. Malka now suggested we exchange photos. On receiving her picture, I said "not bad." In retrospect, the photographer should have been rewarded with an Oscar for cinematography.

Finally, Malka proposed coming to Israel during her school's summer vacation. I arranged to meet her at the airport, and at once discovered this photographic apparition. Well, a deal's a deal, and I always liked to think of myself as a gentleman. As we approached my car, this conversation ensued.

Malka: "Yechezkel, I should tell you now. I have a problem with cars and drivers. Until I gain confidence in the driver, I have to sit in the car looking out the back window.

Yechezkel: "And if you never acquire this sense of confidence?"

Malka: "Then if you don't mind, I'll have to sit on the car floor in the back."

Needless to say, I drove the 25 miles back to Jerusalem from Ben Gurion *very* carefully. There was more, but that would just be loshen hora. Malka was quickly scratched off the list of contenders.

Perhaps this story would pale in comparison with the Los Angeles shidduch with a former member of Hell's Angels motorcyclists. Now a Lubavitcher, but still dressed in black leather apparel.

Episode #3

Finally, I found an ad in the Jerusalem Post personals column.

DRW (Divorced religious woman); new oleh from middle America; two grown daughters.

OK, lets see what this is about. I called the telephone number. A lady answered. We quickly discovered a common denominator; her family was in the scrap business in Cincinnati. Fran (not her real name) had arrived here two months ago. She still resided in the mercaz klita (absorption center) in Gilo, Jerusalem. To spare us the embarrassment of a public meeting in the mercaz klita reception hall, we decided she would be standing at a telephone booth outside the center. As I drove up at the appointed hour, I was overwhelmed. I didn't know which was larger in overall bulk – the phone booth or Fran. (Plus I have a small Fiat.) I started to drive away. But my conscience was sitting on my shoulder and talking in my ear. (You know the picture! The mitzvah is "V'ahavta l'rayacha k'mocha" – love your neighbor like yourself.) I was trapped by my years of mussar[1] and Torah study. I took a deep breath and turned the car around. My mind began to work overtime; where is a secluded, dark place to take this Amazon. The evening was a torture chamber.

---

1. mussar – ethical and religious instruction.

There are dozens more tales, some pleasant, others often depressing, and some hilarious. To summarize, I will certify that those who find a true mate in life, an aishes chayil,[1] are blessed. Don't feel you are missing something; there is *nothing out there*, in most cases, but pain, anxiety and disappointment.

Recently, I attended a seminar presented by a young American rabbi. I think his words are worth recording. "I oftentimes am the officiating rabbi at weddings. Standing under the chupah (marriage canopy) you wish to say something meaningful to the newly married couple. I tell them the ring they exchanged symbolically is another link in the chain of Jewish families going back over 4,000 years, from the marriage of Abraham to Sarah."

In my case, I have added another five links without even planning to do so!

---

1. aishes chayil – woman of valor.

THE HYNDA STORY
WIFE #4

This occurred during my visit to the States in the summer of 1979. Dr. Joe Ingber was an old pal from my years in Whitestone, Queens, New York City, during my second marriage. Joe was sharing a vacation home in West Hampton, Long Island. We made contact, and he invited me out for a day. We had been keen competitors in every possible sport – bowling, golf, tennis, pitching coins, you name it. But good pals, nevertheless.

Joe arranged a tennis game at a friend's luxurious home in the area, with a private tennis court and full-size pool. Awaiting our turn to play, I heard a woman calling after her dog, "Malka! Malka!" I called out, "Do you know that means 'Queen' in Hebrew?" Hynda replied, "Of course. In fact I recently returned from a vacation in Israel."

A brief history of Hynda, the daughter of two Shoah survivors. They were a hard-working couple, and over the years had accumulated modest wealth in the retail business. They resided in the Bronx. Like most Jewish parents, they wanted their children to have a better life than they had. Their son, Isaac, became a teacher and eventually, a successful real estate investor. Hynda, somewhat embarrassed by her parents' poor English and conversation (they were basically Yiddish speakers) and un-American traits, worked to distance herself from her roots. She took acting and dancing lessons, attended Music and Art High School in New York City, and a New England university, Tufts. Broadway was not prepared to receive her contribution to their world. As a result, Hynda became a high school English teacher. There ensued several unsuccessful relationships with both Jews and gentiles. As an example, there was an extended affair with a sixth generation New England American gentleman, obviously a statement about her activities and direction. He eventually sent her a "Dear John" letter from Vietnam.

At that point in my own life story I was at the Diaspora Yeshiva – as described fully elsewhere – and on leaving for the States Rabbi Goldstein, properly urged me to look for a shidduch. I was 53 and had been single for several years. On impulse, I asked Hynda for her phone number. I called when I returned to New York City. As I was leaving in a few days, I asked when we could meet. I was now Shabbos observant and leaving that next Sunday night. It seemed that we only had Saturday evening.

Hynda: "I already have a late Saturday night date to go dancing. You can be my early Saturday night date." I visited her East 73rd apartment. We chatted for an hour, and I dutifully left, prior to her *real* Saturday night date.

On my return to Jerusalem and the yeshiva, the Rabbi asked, "Nu, how did you succeed in the shidduch department?"

Y: "Rabbi, I met two possible shidduchim. One, on the plane going, a divorcee with three grown children. On visiting her home I discovered she was a wealthy divorcee under treatment by a shrink several times a week. I crossed her off the list quickly. The second has somewhat greater possibility. But she is involved in the New York City Big Apple Scene."

RG: "Yechezkel, do yourself a favor. Sit down and write her a simple postal card saying:

Dear Hynda,

The Big Apple excitement is all about getting turned on.
    When you're involved in the Torah world, you're tuned in constantly. Therefore, no highs and lows!

Just sign your name and address."

When at the yeshiva, you accept the Rabbi's judgment implicitly. So, I did just that, and sent it off to Hynda in the Big Apple. And soon forgot the entire episode.

The clock moves forward six months. Surprisingly, I received a lengthy letter from Hynda. I will attempt to reconstruct it as nearly as I can remember.

Dear Yechezkel,

I received your card last summer and stuck it on the mirror of my dressing table. I've been viewing it daily. Here it's New Year's Eve 1980. I'm well into my 30's and have been tossed about in many relationships and going nowhere. I'd like to investigate your suggestion of getting *tuned in*.

Best Wishes,

Happy New Year
Hynda

So began an intense correspondence and phone call relationship. In several months, during her school Easter break, Hynda visited Jerusalem. I exposed her to my life and detailed my history. Oddly, Basil Anderman of the Anderman Tales was visiting at the same time, with his escort, Judy.

A case of D. I. occurred here, I'm certain. Basil was on an extensive tour. They had first visited interior Africa on a rich man's safari. We met when he checked into the Jerusalem Hilton. That evening I had been invited to the Roths for the Pesach Seder, with Hynda. I called the ever-generous Roths and told them about Basil. They said sure, bring him along. As I prepared to leave my house for the visitors and Hynda, I received an urgent call. Basil was ill. We all sped to the Hadassah emergency ward. Basil was shaking and feverish. The skeleton staff at Hadassah (on Seder night) heard his story of the African visit and deduced he had contracted a virus that his body could not fight off. All the time sitting in the emergency room "Dear Judy" sat complaining about their plans and itinerary, now upset. It turned out my friend had a liver infection and stayed overnight at the hospital. We arrived at the Roths about midnight.

At the same time, I had been suffering from an enlarged boil on my rear end. My appointment to see a specialist was chol hamoed Pesach (the intermediate days of Pesach), the next day. When Professor Ayal (who is now my neighbor in the Old City) examined me he said, "I want you in surgery tomorrow, 8:00 a.m. I don't like the look of that 'growth'." We all know what that infers.

In the morning, I picked up Hynda. By 8:30 I was in surgery. The growth was promptly removed and I was left to "sweat" the rest of the day, waiting for the biopsy. Dear Hynda and Judy, not wishing to spoil *their* respective vacations, went touring and had an enjoyable lunch. Any normal person should have recognized this episode for what it was: two self-indulgent women, concerned only with the pursuit of pleasure – the *Me* syndrome. Well, Basil and I both recovered. He entertained Judy for several years and then set her adrift. Yechezkel, the idiot, did not recognize the D.I. symbolism and married Hynda that summer in the Jerusalem Hilton in another extravaganza.

I covered a significant part of the Hynda story in an opening section, "The Apartment."

To tie all the loose ends together, I returned to the States. In a few months we announced our intention to marry. Her parents promised us the marriage would not last four months; they miscalculated – it lasted four difficult years. Only her mother came for the wedding. I found out subsequently it was in order to transfer Hynda's part ownership in several properties back to the family. They thought I was marrying her for her wealth!

Where to her as a tourist everything looked quaint and exciting, living here in Israel and experiencing the many daily inconveniences and discomforts were too much for Hynda, who was no longer a tourist, but now a resident. In the meantime, I was herded like a prize bull with my sperm samples to a number of laboratories in Israel and the States to find out why Hynda had not conceived. In spite of my having three beautiful, healthy children, the implication was my sperm were getting lazy.

In the end, Hynda rejected my Orthodox Jewish lifestyle that she had vowed to uphold. She got to hate the inconveniences of living here. She maintained her New York City apartment by subleasing it, so when the final split occurred, she returned to the Big Apple uninjured. I ultimately discovered that during her frequent buying trips to the States to restock her shmatta and hat business, she had met a lawyer, whom she married shortly after our divorce. Still unable to conceive, she adopted a daughter, and the last I heard, she had also divorced husband #2, the attorney.

As for this stud bull, he was put back out to pasture. It seems his sperm count was still adequate.

ONLY IN ISRAEL
#9

For the past 15 years I've maintained a P. O. Box in Beit Hakerem, Jerusalem. Some ten years ago the following incident occurred.

There is a slight ramp of perhaps ten degrees leading up to the post office. While I was returning to my car after checking my box, an obviously physically impaired, aged woman was being assisted down the ramp by a middle-aged woman. As I passed, the younger woman called, "Slach li (excuse me), could you take the other arm of this ailing grandmother." In response, I clutched the other arm. Amazingly, the previous helper suddenly let go of her side and ran off. I was left holding grandma's frail arm.

We continued shuffling – not walking – in progressions of 4 to 6 inches. When we finally reached the sidewalk, I asked, "Grandma, are you beseder (OK) now?" She replied, "I have to go downtown."

YM: "In your condition?"

Grandma: "Do you want to do the mitzvah?" (In Yiddish.) With this, I pulled my car close to the curb and assisted her inside with considerable difficulty.

YM: "Where downtown?"

Grandma: "Jaffa Road and King George." The heart of the city. On arrival, I had to stop traffic to allow her to exit, again with much difficulty.

Grandma: "I feel faint. Can you get me something to drink?"

YM: "Water?"

Grandma: "No, carrot juice."

Yechezkel purchased a cup of carrot juice, placed her leaning against a building and drove off.

Lesson: At times it's difficult to do even a small mitzvah.

YECHEZKEL MINK, THE BANKER

In retelling the tales of my misadventure in the scrap business, I related how I soon ran out of working capital. I had put all my cash into fixed assets. Thinking I was still in the States, I presented my investment to the manager at Barclay's Discount in Tel Aviv. He responded, "This is not collateral. If you go broke, what can we do with this pile of steel?" I raced back to New York and, fortunately, was directed to a vice-president at Bank Leumi, New York, who agreed to guarantee my notes as a line of credit in Israel. This person was David Crohn, who saved my backside temporarily till I closed down the Israeli operation.

I had just married Hynda, and was no longer interested in my P. R. position at the Diaspora Yeshiva. (Covered in the chapter on the Diaspora Yeshiva.) Surprisingly, I discovered an announcement and photo in the Jerusalem Post. The same Dave Crohn who helped me five years earlier was now in Jerusalem, as head of Tourist Banking services for Bank Leumi. I went to visit him as a good friend. Dave was really pleased to see me.

DC: "What happened to your scrap business?"

YM: "Down the tubes."

DC: "What a pity. Did you pay back the bank?"

YM: "Every agora."

DC: "So what are you doing now?"

YM: "Well, I have been studying at the Diaspora Yeshiva the past two years and also doing P. R. work for them."

DC: "What a waste of talent. Come work for me at the bank."

YM: "My Hebrew is inadequate."

DC: "You won't be working with Israelis; mainly tourists, English speakers."

I took the job on the spot.

Crohn took care of all the bureaucratic BS and I was assigned to work initially at the two-man office at the King David, then the Jerusalem Hilton, and finally, the Plaza, which basically was my venue for 3½ years.

Tourists would arrive with loads of Israel Bonds which, within certain parameters, they could cash in Israel for their expenses – and pocket money. My job (I didn't need Hebrew) was to convince them to open a dollar savings account here. This would still allow them to keep the money in Israel, and earn much higher interest rates than taking the money back to their home country. (It would still aid our economy.) True to Crohn's appreciation of my salesmanship abilities, in a few months I was the star salesman of dollar accounts in Jerusalem. Within six months, I was giving seminars (in English) on banking in Israel. My salary was meager, at best. But I enjoyed the job. It served two purposes; it rekindled my Zionist bent and also relit a fire under my commercial capabilities.

1983-4 saw a major reversal of fortunes in Israel's economy in general, and the banking and economy here. For several years in the early 80's, we had seen a balloon economy constantly inflating. The stock market was constantly rising, especially the bank stocks, which the banks aided by supporting the bank share Market. Every six months they would issue additional stock, which would be over-subscribed by twenty or thirty times. Remember, everything was highly inflated and leveraged. We employees were issued stock option purchase rights which were promptly executed at a profit. It was great. It would never stop. Well, suddenly, one day the banks ran out of liquidity. The chairman at Bank Hapoalim committed suicide. Our chairman at Bank Leumi ran for a safe haven to America. All were indicted for fraud. The trial ran for years. None of the major actors served time. The Israeli government had to provide billions of dollars to stabilize the banking system; and in a major reversal of expansion, all the small hotel branches were closed. Yechezkel was out of a job again. Just like Papa fifty years ago, a victim of the depression.

The job was basically a transitional experience for me and very enjoyable. Dave Crohn returned to New York and retired shortly after. We still meet on occasion, in Jerusalem. I bank at the new tourist center branch next to the King David Hotel and maintain a camaraderie with many of my former co-workers.

BATSHEVA
WIFE #5

As previously noted, when I married Gloria at age 22, I could never have imagined I'd be at a station to choose a fifth wife. But life is an adventure and often unpredictable. There I stood, divorced from Hynda, wife #4, and facing the prospect of living alone (really unbearable), or perhaps taking another marital fling. It had been a period of four years; there had been several relationships but none reached fruition. I came to a decision: Obviously I needed another methodology for choosing a mate. I carefully designed a list of qualifications for this very desirable position, in which longevity was a major question mark.

Hence my list of priorities:

1. A seriously religiously committed woman, who could join me at my level of religious observance.
2. A woman willing to cover her hair after marriage as is the norm in the Orthodox community.
3. Her resolve to live in Israel permanently.
4. To reside in the Old City, Jerusalem, at my home.
5. A non-smoker.
6. No intention of maintaining an animal in our home.
7. She should have an occupation or full-time vocation.
8. I required the approval of my rabbi, Mordechai Scheinberger, *schlita*.[1]
   Perhaps to the outsider, this might be absurd. But looking at my track

---

1. denoting respect for a learned rabbi.

record, these were the areas of former impasses. Incidentally, I had previously arrived with other candidates, but the Rabbi had subtly suggested we should wait and evaluate.

The Shidduch[1]

I met BatSheva via a shidduch suggested by a neighbor, Chaya Bracha Perlstein, who spoke to me one day on the street.

CBP: "Tell me, Mr. Mink, do you ever intend to remarry, or will you remain single?"

YM: "I definitely do not want to remain single."

CBP: "I believe I have someone you should meet."

Several weeks passed. Mrs. Perlstein called one evening.

CBP: "There's a divorced woman here in the Jewish Quarter who might also be searching for a mate."

Chaya Bracha's presentation was so laudatory that I remarked, "Why set up a meeting; just tell her to meet me under the chupah!" She laughed and gave me BatSheva's telephone number.

That same evening I called. BatSheva sounded positive and I suggested we meet. She asked, when? I responded, "Why not now?" That evening, we met at a designated location in the Old City, about 200 meters from my home. BatSheva also owned an apartment in the area. She arrived with her dog. Problem #1. But aside from the animal, she appeared normal. (Note previous chapter on odd people in the Single Scene.) I invited her up for a cup of tea and conversation. She readily accompanied me and did not object when I said, "Leave the dog outside." Our conversation lasted an hour. I related a bit of my history – *a very small portion*. She also gave me an overview of her life story.

BatSheva's Story

BatSheva had arrived in Israel with two young daughters six years prior to our meeting. She was widowed in her 20's, when her husband died of cancer. He was just 35.

---

1. shidduch – an arranged meeting towards marriage.

The struggle to overcome the illness and costly treatments had decimated their savings – which left her with only one possession – an abandoned farm they had bought on a lark in the farming county of Sussex, England. BatSheva had always enjoyed the outdoors and had an interest in gardening, with a real green thumb.

Born in London's East End, she was a victim of a hasty marriage in wartime England between a fortunate German Jewish mother of the kindertransport[1] and a British Jewish soldier. After the war, BatSheva's mother left the marriage to join her brother, a survivor of the death camps, who was now living in Brooklyn, New York. Those two were the only survivors of ten children. BatSheva and her brother, Phillip, came to the States with their mother, Helen. The father remained in England and they formally divorced several years later. Helen, her mother, subsequently married a distant cousin, Jossel. BatSheva never liked the States, and returned to England in her late teens. She met her future husband and remained there.

Finding herself alone in the world with two small children and this decrepit farm and abandoned farmhouse, BatSheva slowly rebuilt her life, with the aid of a modest widow's pension. Utilizing a scheme financed by the British Government to bring the people back to the land via a work/study farming technology program also helped. Over a period of ten years she converted this disaster into a successful enterprise, growing vegetables and flowers under glass.

In spite of zero knowledge of Jewish religion or practices, she felt alone, as there were no Jewish residents in the community, and BatSheva experienced a rootless existence. Prior to the decision to make aliyah (after selling the farm), there was a brief six-month marriage and divorce in England to a Jewish M.D. On arrival in Israel, another three-month marriage to an Israeli former policeman failed. Shortly after (with the money from the sale of her farm), she purchased a home in the Old City and found a job at a beginner's salary with the Botanical Gardens at the Hebrew University. After years of deprivation and struggle, along came Yechezkel.

---

1. kindertransport – children brought from German-occupied areas to safer locations throughout Europe.

I walked her home that first evening, returned home, and lay awake reviewing the evening's events. BatSheva fitted almost all my criteria and it seemed I'd probably never find a better fit; we all know there is no perfect match.

The Proposal

The next afternoon I called. (BatSheva had told me her work day was from 6 a.m. till 2 p.m.).

Y: "I'd like to come over for a few minutes; it's a very important matter, and besides, I have a date this evening with another woman."

BatSheva: "I'll be ready in half an hour; but what's so important?"

Y (on arrival): "I've been thinking it over since last night. I think we should get married."

She was shocked, to put it mildly.

BatSheva: "We hardly know each other."

Y: "I have a list of requirements and you seem to fit the bill almost completely."

BatSheva: "I also have a requirement. I need a man with a sense of humor and you must have one or you must be crazy, proposing after a one hour meeting! In addition, I request you accompany me and spend a day at my work in the gardens."

(Her previous husband objected to her unfeminine job, and demanded she resign it, over her sorrowful objections. However, he left after a few months, pursuing another flirtation, and BatSheva regained her position, where she is employed today.)

After the proposal, I promptly left to keep my previous date. On my arrival, the woman announced she was ill (perhaps of me). I quickly exited and returned to BatSheva. I explained the circumstances of my quick return, and over a cup of tea suggested we marry promptly. The next morning I picked her up at 6 a.m. to go to work in the gardens. I spent the day helping out; we also planted two small saplings, symbolic of our new beginning. We then discussed the issue of her dog, which really was the possession of her children who had returned to England for their own reasons. BatSheva advertised and gave it away.

That evening, together we visited the home of my rabbi, Mordechai Scheinberger, *schlita*, for his approval.

RS: "Yechezkel, how long have you known BatSheva?"

Y: "Two days."

RS, half laughing, but maintaining a state of decorum: "Do you think this is the shidduch you require to finally settle down and resume a family life?"

Y: "I really think so, Rabbi."

That conversation took place all in Yiddish. He then turned to BatSheva with several questions about her background and family in Hebrew. (Her Hebrew is superior to mine.) Rabbi Scheinberger then looked at me, his twinkling blue eyes laughing, and announced, 'It's Beseder'! (I approve.) We both respectfully thanked him and left.

We promptly ran into old pal and friend, Rabbi Gedalia Gurfein (of *Seven Beggars* fame).

I introduced him to BatSheva. He inquired, "What's new?"

I said, "Not a great deal; however, we're getting married next week."

Now Gedalia was in shock. We invited him up to BatSheva's home (which was nearer) and we three drank a lechaim.[1]

The Wedding

In the opening of the Bialystok Visit chapter, I discussed the annual Kerman-sponsored Thanksgiving Day dinner of the Gering (Blumberg) side of my family. With Thanksgiving only three weeks away, it seemed best we should marry promptly and meet most of my family in one session. In Israel, the first step in the marriage procedure is to open a file in the Rabbinate. (I knew; I had already done it twice.) Since we had both been married and divorced in Jerusalem previously, I assumed they would have the files. BatSheva knew better. When we applied, she brought her divorce papers. I couldn't put my hand on mine at that moment.

---

1. lechaim – a good luck toast.

Meet the Talmudic Mind

BatSheva was approved at once. To me the Rabbi said, "Yes, we have your records, but without the original documents you must appear before a Beit Din (Rabbinic Court), a process of perhaps a month." Reason: you might have used the get to marry in another country. In my case this was a definite possibility. I was beside myself; where could those papers be? Again Divine Intervention appears. It obviously was stored in my subconscious. That night, I got up from a deep sleep at 3 or 4 a.m. and walked directly over to a bookshelf where I had my get buried in a book. Really amazing.

The next morning we arrived together at the Rabbinate with all the documents. A new impasse: According to Rabbinic ordinance, you had to wait thirteen days between filing and marriage, I assume in the event some negative evidence of misrepresentation appeared. However!!! If you request a special bypassing of this Rabbinic by-law by the Chief Rabbi of your city, you may proceed. We appeared the next morning before Chief Rabbi Kolitz of Jerusalem and explained the situation; tznius (modesty) demanded we should not travel out of the country together. After a 5-minute deliberation with his aides, he gave us approval to waive the thirteen-day interval.

Now you can understand how I lost my temper in the Only in Israel chapters of small-minded bureaucrats as I proceeded from desk to desk, official to official.

The next morning we began inviting friends to the wedding which took place in my home on the mirpesset (terrace) overlooking the Kotel (Western Wall). It was a memorable event, attended by about 50 people.

Gloria Kramer, a neighbor, took over the impromptu catering and arrangements. Gloria has always shown herself to be a remarkable and capable friend, wife of my friend Michael, mother of five children, and now the grandmother of no less than 28 grandchildren. My Rabbi Scheinberger performed the Kiddushim (marriage ceremony). The marriage is now nine years old. As BatSheva says, she is presently in the #2 position in longevity and going for the world record (still held by Gloria M., of 15 years.) Time alone will tell.

Finally, BatSheva is a survivor and a very giving, honest individual, which is a very positive concern of mine.

ONLY IN ISRAEL
#10

The experience of dealing with the small-minded bureaucrats and their procedures I have never been able to overcome, even after twenty years. Nine years ago, when BatSheva and I decided to marry after a *very* short incubation period (nine days), the frustrations were unbearable. First, we had to appear before Chief Rabbi of Jerusalem, Reb Kolitz, and explain why we couldn't wait the required two weeks. Now began a tour of small offices, each with a rubber stamp, or pasted-on stamp. Each station calls for a small fee, which employs another clerk selling stamps, or imprinting rubber stamps. Finally, we came to the last station (a stamp to be purchased). The clerk was on a coffee break from his stressful work load. I sat patiently for ten or fifteen minutes, trying to contain my frustration and impatience with these outmoded procedures. Finally, the stamp seller appeared. As I approached him to buy the stamp, another individual jumped in front. Placing his case on the seller's desk, he yelled out, "Shmuel, ma nishma?" (How are you?) He also had to buy the same mandatory stamps. I stopped him short: "S'licha, I'm on line first, Sir!"

His reply: "I'm an important attorney; I come here every day." And dismissed me as irrelevant.

Y.M.: "I've been standing 15 minutes."

The attorney continued to speak non-stop to Shmuel, opening his wallet to buy the stamps. At this point, the long repressed Jerry Mink, the Junkman, surfaced. I snatched his briefcase. He continued to ignore me. With one motion, I threw it against the wall. Out poured the contents: 1 sandwich, 1 banana, 1 orange, and several files. He looked at me astounded. "You must be crazy."

Y.M.: "Yes, I'm crazy, and I get these seizures whenever donkeys like you jump the line."

I promptly purchased the required third set of stamps. The next day we were married.

MY OPINION ABOUT CHASSIDIM
AND THEIR CUSTOMS

We Jews have been in the diaspora for 2,000 years. It is only with D.I. that we are once again in our homeland, having lost countless millions on the road back. As a fellow returnee to Israel for the past twenty years, I'm fascinated by the various groups – each arriving with its own customs, eating habits, languages, religious ritual, and wearing apparel (even we Americans). The most controversial, in my opinion, are the Chassidim of Central Europe.

Originally followers of the Baal Shem Tov, a 17th century leader, they continue clothing themselves in dress, as someone once remarked, worn by Polish-Russian aristocrats of the 17-18th century. Why the fur hats and striped pants and coats? Some walk with black rounded shoes, others with white stockings under the ⅔-length pants legs. Payot – I've seen men with side curls 12 or 15 inches long, etc., etc. And of course long black coats at all times.

I'm also trying very hard to be an observant Jew. Pray tell, what have these outfits to do with religious respect for our Creator? I know tradition; I also want to live and let live. But this is the ingathering; why not leave these practices behind? It's incredible, during the height of the summer, with temperatures in the 90's here in Israel, to see grown men and boys confined under layers of dark clothing and topped by a huge fur streimel – did Moshe Rabbeinu wear one?

I know all the standard answers. We wish to be identified with our sect of Judaism. But do we still need sects? I know we were once twelve tribes. But now we are all one group, except for the Levites and the Kohanim who have special duties to perform in religious practice and according to our Torah, in the Third Temple when it will be rebuilt (with Hashem's help).

I can only assign to these clothing fashion slaves a title one of my rabbi teachers assigned them: Marching Morons.

In juxtaposition, allow me to share with you another thought. The two outstanding rabbinic figures in my life presently, are my rebbe, Reb Mordechai Scheinberger *schlita*, a man with whom I daven all year round. He is a tzaddik, truly worthy of the name "chussid" (for kindness). He is my advisor, friend, and counselor, in times of difficulties.

There is a concept understood within the Orthodox world: the continued existence of the world is maintained by the lamed-vovnikim. Of these thirty-six individuals – we never know who they are – I believe one could be Reb Mordechai. He comes closest of anyone I have met personally. Secondly, Rabbi Gottlieb, whom I described in my opening chapter (Divine Intervention), another individual I respect highly. Also a chussid. So there is my problem. How do I reconcile these two positions? My total respect of these two Chassidim with my ongoing sense of the irrationality of these costumes?

THE GEMACH
(INTEREST-FREE LOAN FUND)

It all began some sixty years ago. I remember as a boy that Tuesday night was achtse[1] night for Papa. Now that I know a bit of Hebrew, I suppose the word means "brotherhood" in a Yiddish derivation.

On occasion I would go with Papa to the achtse meetings. They were coordinated by the same Mr. Sam Shapiro, the accountant and administrator mentioned previously. Money had been loaned from a commercial institution and additional funds added by the members. The purpose was to make monies available for needy individuals who could not apply to banks for lack of credit standing. As I recall, the weekly report was given by Mr. Shapiro and new applicants were interviewed. All the formal activities took place above a catering facility in Brownsville, Brooklyn, and were completed in 15-20 minutes. Then the real business of the evening would begin. The table was cleared for action, i.e., the weekly card game. Mr. Shapiro would leave with the books, coffee was served, and applicants departed. Jerry Mink would watch the game for a few hours and go home after consuming a quantity of goodies, half asleep. P. S. The loans were repaid with interest to cover loan expenses and Mr. Shapiro was reimbursed for his work.

Shortly after I became active with the Diaspora Yeshiva, I recognized the financial distress most of the students lived in, barely scraping through from one Shabbos to the next. In a real financial crisis, life was a total disaster. On my own, I returned to the States and, by some good fortune, collected $8,500,

---

1. achtse – brotherhood.

which I gave over to a committee to execute loans when needed. ($5,000 of the money was given by one individual as covered in another chapter – Givers and Takers.) When I left the yeshiva 1½ years later, the money was untraceable. I'm definitely not accusing anyone of malfeasance; it was a case of financial irresponsibility and lack of capable management. The $8,500 disappeared down the drain of chessed and tzedaka.

Eight years ago, I was discussing with my friend and neighbor, Mike Kramer, our financial losses resulting from local people coming to both of us for loans, and our resultant inability to recover the money. He told the tale of loaning a local $875 and that person now avoiding him. I also was the victim of several such experiences.

I suggested that the situation could be remedied if it was operated in a business-like fashion, with forms and guarantors, and post-dated checks. His initial contribution was the aforementioned $875 and I matched it. We eventually each contributed $3,000. Let me proudly report that our keren (fund) now boasts a balance of $250,000 in loans outstanding. All the monies were contributed by charitable individuals and one major institution (Keren Klita).

We are currently primarily involved with the neediest element of our society – the flood of Russian olim who have entered Israel over the last eight years. I supervise the arrangements of loans and collections. The number of loans made as of December 1996 are in excess of 800 and I can proudly state we have not, to date, written off one bad debt, though several have required years of effort to recoup, and even litigation.

This is not an ego trip, but a statement of fact. I seem to have an ability to deal with the complexities of 180-200 rotating loans very easily. (Remember Mink the Mariner – arithmetic superstar!) It is a gift I possess of memory and facility with numbers, plus a drive *not* to give up in pursuing the few rotten apples or "deadbeats." (One of the minor mishaps is reported in another chapter.)

But as consequence of 900 loans, a book could also be written covering those events. Incidentally, 35 loans have been repaid by guarantors, usually under pressure. In summary, the gemach now consumes at least ten hours a week of my time. But in reflection, hopefully when I approach the Table of

Decision at the end of my days here in this world, perhaps the angel in charge of gemachim will step forward to say a good word for me and my partner, the donation administrator, Mike Kramer, for the good deeds we have done. In my case, I hope my work has helped in eradicating any averas (transgressions) that I committed in this world.

ADVENTURES ON THE GEMACH TRAIL

The Scam

One Friday morning we received a call from a young man whose voice sounded distressful. His mother was in the hospital and needed emergency surgery. The surgeon would not operate without a substantial down payment on his fee of $4,000 – at least $1,500 equivalent in Israeli shekels on account.

Me: "Can't we wait until our regular meeting on Tuesday night?"

He: "Don't you understand, it's an emergency!"

I suggested that we meet at a hotel and that he bring along his guarantors and a series of checks to cover repayment. That part went off well. Fortunately, we met on a Friday afternoon – after bank closing. That Motzae Shabbos, I met socially with Mr. & Mrs. R., two of our generous donors. To give them some nachas, I relayed the epic of Saving Mom.

R., being astute and interested, asked, "What hospital?"

Stumped and feeling insecure, I called first thing Sunday morning, 7 a.m., to inquire as to Mom's condition and what hospital.

To my chagrin, who answered? Mom!

Me: "How do you feel?"

Mom: "Wonderful, thank you."

I dropped everything and arrived at the bank in time to be first in line at the opening. I forewarned the chief teller and everyone else I could find to stop payment on our check. Baruch Hashem, the check was stopped and I met several days later with our con maven to return his checks.

This is only one of countless experiences. Others will be related in the forthcoming book, *Adventures on the Gemach Trail*.

GIVERS AND TAKERS

In dealing with the mitzvohs of loaning, giving charity or performing acts of chessed (kindness), to quote the Chofetz Chaim, for the givers there are no questions. For the non-givers, there are no answers. This has also been my experience.

Givers

In the mid-1960's I resided with my family in affluent East Hills, a Roslyn, LI, NY suburb, in an area of rolling hills and formidable stately homes. Ninety percent of the residents were Jewish and I suppose snobbish – we all know the scene: look at my home, car, garden, children, clothes. A clan of typical, successful, competitive Jews. As previously discerned, on the social and business level I was on the lowest rung; 1. My family tree foliage lacked prominence – "yichus."[1] 2. My profession as a junkman was definitely not impressive. 3. Plus, I was merely 30 years old when we entered this stratosphere; but I paid cash for my home.

In time, we joined the local Conservative synagogue, bowling teams, even, after a few years, a golf club (a definite social ascent). The development had a private swimming pool and tennis courts. What does one usually talk about while sitting around the pool? Loshen hora! Also known as negative stories about others. One summer the grist in the rumor mill was the financial

---

1. Yichus – religious respectability.

difficulties of a neighbor, George Freed (not his name). One summer afternoon, I arrived at the pool and found George and his family sunning themselves.

J. Mink: "George, how are you? I've heard much talk about your current financial problems."

G. Freed: "It's true, Jerry. I've had some serious reversals and am really struggling at this point."

J. Mink: "George, don't be embarrassed. If you need a modest short-term loan, please call and let me know."

G. Freed: "Jerry, I can't tell you how much I appreciate your offer. Not one of my supposed S.O.B. friends has come forward to help."

George never called.

The clock spins forward 15 years. The ba'al teshuva, Yechezkel Mink, decides to establish a keren (gemach) to assist Diaspora Yeshiva students. I arrived in the States and received a mixed reception, calling on family, former friends and business associates. During a visit to a former pal from East Hills, LI, NY, we spoke about what happened to my former neighbors: who's divorced (like me), doing well financially, doing poorly, all probably loshen hora. The former neighbor informed me that our mutual friend, George Freed, had experienced a total reversal of fortune again and was now thriving financially. He even supplied his new company name and address. Having nothing to lose, I called.

George Freed: "Jerry, what happened to you? I heard that you were divorced and then ran off to Israel. How are you?"

Y. Mink: "George, I'm fine, I'd like to visit you at the office."

G. Freed: "Definitely come out. I'd really be pleased to see you."

The revamped J. Mink, now Yechezkel, a ba'al teshuva with kippa and tzitzis, entered George's obviously prosperous establishment.

G. Freed, on seeing the *new me*, "What happened to you? Are you a rabbi now?"

Y. Mink: "No, George, merely an Orthodox, observant Jew with a new lifestream and direction."

G. Freed: "What can I do for you? I'm pressed for time; I have to be in Washington, DC, this evening."

I gave him the pitch about 40 yeshiva students, many with large families, continually in need of loans.

G. Freed: "How much do you want?"

Y. Mink: "George, don't put me on the spot."

G. Freed: "I have to leave. Give me an amount or see me again next time you're in the States."

I swallowed hard, again feeling I had nothing to lose, and said, $5,000.

George picked up the phone to his secretary. "Ellen, bring my checkbook. This 'rabbi' will give you a name, I'll sign the check. I have to leave. So long, Jerry. Good seeing you again." Perhaps I should have said $10,000!?!

Takers

I was doing business in Woodside, Queens, and one day was called on by a scrap aluminum buyer for a major consumer. I invited him to lunch. He began relating his personal financial difficulties: five children, sick wife, salary barely covering his daily living expenses, in significant financial distress. He also indicated if I helped him he could clue me into market trends. I agreed to loan him several thousand dollars. Yes, he'd repay it monthly – $300 a month – and I would be saving his marriage and extricating him from major disaster.

The first month, Bob (not his name) failed to appear. I called and instead of $300, I received $100 in the mail. The second month I had to call and did not receive a response or money. By the third month, I was getting angry at him and myself as well. Finally I told him, if he doesn't come over and start to make restitution, I would call his employers and complain. The next day he came with his young son, about five years old.

Bob: "Tell me, Jerry, do your children have shoes? My son is walking nearly barefoot." He showed me the tattered sandals on his son's feet.

With that, he threw $50 on my desk, shouting, "Here, take this. Now you can throw it away on some trivia." I begged him to retrieve the $50 and buy the boy a pair of shoes. I realize now I was the victim of a scam. It's happened so many times over the years. I've come to realize the perpetrators of these maneuvers can sense their victims miles away.

Givers

In the Moshe Golan Ripoff chapter, I mentioned the Capra Brothers of Brescia, Italy, a successful and honorable scrap aluminum consumer. I discovered subsequently that they had a silent partner, Zeev Eisicovic, of Vienna, Austria, who had very significant business connections behind the Iron Curtain for buying scrap to supply their smelting operation. Eventually I began trading with Capra, but could not cover the money seepage of the Golan problem, and then the Aviva divorce settlement (chapter: Aviva, Wife #3), etc. With my line of credit fully extended, and my checks becoming non-negotiable, I went to the States, desperate for help. Nothing was forthcoming. On the way back to Israel, really depressed, I stopped in Vienna to investigate the possibility of additional business with Capra. Zeev (a Shoah survivor, and, following WWII, a kibbutznik in Israel) welcomed me warmly at his home and office outside Vienna.

Zeev: "Jerry, I heard you are having a very difficult time."

I gave him a 5-minute replay of the current scenario.

Zeev: "Would $25,000 help you?"

JM: "Definitely; I've nowhere else to turn."

He took out his checkbook, wrote a check on a Swiss bank account, and handed it to me.

JM: "Where are the papers to sign?"

Zeev: "Papers are worthless. I've learned to judge people, not papers."

It took two years, but I was able to repay every cent.

WHAT IS VENEZUELA, SABA?

In my opinion, a threatening phenomenon is occurring among the children of the Ba'alei Teshuva Movement.

Many thousands of educated and newly religious people from the West have, after making aliyah, begun families – usually large – and elected to send their offspring to schools that educate almost entirely in Torah learning. This denies their children exposure to general knowledge their parents received. Recently, I visited a friend, formerly a successful American businessman, now retired and surrounded here in Israel by a large number of grandchildren. The grandfather (also now a ba'al teshuva[1]) often boasts with pride of the abilities of his grandchildren to delve into complex gemarahs, their commentaries (pilpul), as well as quoting verbatim vast sections of chumash. While talking one evening in generalities, the name Venezuela came up. Asked the obviously bright teen-aged Talmud student grandson and teenager who was sitting with us:

Teen: "Saba, what is Venezuela?"

Saba: "That's a country in South America."

Teen: "What is South America?"

Saba: "That's a continent south of North America."

Teen: "What's North America?"

Saba (becoming irritable and somewhat embarrassed): "That is the continent in which the USA is located."

---

1. ba'al teshuva – literally, master of repentance. One who has become religious.

Teen: "What is a continent?"

Saba: "That is etc., etc., etc."

Parents and friends, there is a world out there beyond Torah. The Torah's importance as a guidebook in life is undeniable. However, our foremost leaders and scholars were also versed in secular information. Moshe Rabbeinu studied in Egyptian schools; the Rambam was a physician and world traveler; Rabbi Schneerson, z"l, went to Sorbonne University and acquired an engineering degree; and so on. How about your offspring. Should they be denied a well-rounded education?

ONLY IN ISRAEL
#11

Spectators often comment on why Israelis are constantly on the run. This episode might help to explain.

For the past 13 years I have driven a battered but serviceable Fiat 127, vintage 1979 (a great year for Fiats). I purchased it third hand, and it has served my purpose of getting around Jerusalem and the Old City wonderfully. I also enjoy keeping it in good operating condition and relish receiving a great deal of kibbitzing about the current level of my economic station via an 18-year-old car. But, as my friend Jerry Hahn wisely noted, "It's not a vehicle but really a hobby!" He has named it the "Minkmobile!"

Seven years ago, the motor died and was replaced. This necessitated notifying the Motor Vehicle Bureau of the replacement of my burned out motor, replaced by a rebuilt one. The repair shop handled the paper work. About a year ago I found the oil consumption of the engine on the rise, while the compression was deteriorating. Yes, time for another motor replacement. I rationalized that after seven years the rebuilt engine owed me nothing. In July 1996, it stopped. I had it towed into my regular repair garage. Unfortunately, friend Yoram Malachi had departed with his family to the States and sold the garage to neophytes. After endless pain and suffering and renting cars, the motor was replaced. Needless to say, without Yoram I returned three times to the garage for additional adjustments. I was finally forced to finish the work at a second garage. The neophytes soon closed the shop and disappeared.

January 1997 was the date for my annual inspection and license renewal (very demanding on an 18-year-old-vehicle). When the tester discovered my motor I.D. number had been changed, the following conversation ensued.

Tester: "Go back to your garage for certification that they changed the motor."

YM: "They are out of business!"

Tester: "Mister, you have a major problem."

YM: "What do I do?"

Tester: "You need an affidavit verifying the facts, signed by your lawyer."

YM: "You mean I have to retain a lawyer?"

Tester: "Yes, that is the only way it can be done."

Perspective

The new self-rule Palestinian State had become a haven for car thieves and chop shops. In 1996 over 30,000 cars were stolen, and most disappeared into the territories. It has now become a major source of revenue for the Palestinians. In fact recently, at a meeting between several Israeli politicians and their Palestinian counterparts, one of the Israelis recognized his stolen car now being driven by a Palestinian official! However, for my rebuilt motor I needed certification!

Back to the saga. Now armed with my original application, lawyer's affidavit, tester's certificate and his list of repairs, I arrived at the Motor Vehicle Office. After a ¾ hour wait to see a clerk, this dialogue evolved.

Clerk (reviewing documentation): "I can't okay this; *only Rochel* can!"

YM: "Where's Rochel?"

Clerk: "Another office."

I was forced to wait for Rochel, the Maven,[1] a half hour. Finally Rochel became available. She reviewed the documents.

Rochel: "I'm not taking responsibility for this. Take it to my supervisor, Mr. Aaron Aaron (not a typing error)."

YM: "Where's Aaron Aaron?"

---

1. maven – expert.

Rochel: "He's gone for the day."

Next morning, I arrived to discover Aaron A. was in the midst of an important meeting. After waiting one hour, I forced my way into the meeting room when someone exited. I discovered the participants at this topflight meeting sitting around a table eating a large salad.

"What's your problem?" he asked, while consuming cucumber slices.

YM: "I need your review of my documents; Rochel will not give her okay."

Aaron A. called Rochel, exchanged some comments, looked me over as though in a police line-up, and directed me back to Rochel, after scribbling something on my application. Rochel now presented a new obstacle: the Bank stamp, for which I had paid the annual fee, was smudged and unclear.

Rochel: "Go back to the bank for a clear affixing of the stamp."

I raced back to the bank. They re-stamped my license form clearly, and a mere three and a half days later I was the proud recipient of a new, yearly registration.

THE SPANISH INQUISITION REVISITED

Two of the new pals who arrived in my life in the last seven years are George and Betsy Kaplan. In 1992, shortly before the Barcelona Olympics, George suggested we assemble a group of men to attend the Events, sharing expenses.

George (henceforth known as "the Organizer") found a travel agency in Jerusalem operated by a Spanish-origin management, International Travels. They arranged for an apartment about 30 miles north of Barcelona, in a town called Ciches (described then as a sleepy fishing village). The agents also supplied five sets of tickets for the sporting events over the two week period, and a rental car. All very expensive, but similar to all joint enterprises when divided by five within financial expedience.

The Partners:

George Kaplan: Jerusalem resident, formerly of Atlanta, Georgia.
Jonathan Kaplan: George's son, New York City.
Jeff Ram: Atlanta resident, soon to make aliyah.
Larry Roth: Jerusalem resident, formerly of Syracuse, NY.
Yours truly: Jerusalem resident.

We decided to pack several Israeli flags in case we found ourselves at sporting events where an Israeli athlete participated. It turned out that at Barcelona, Israel won its first two Olympic medals ever. They were in Judo, which we were not particularly interested in, or ticketed for.

George and I travelled together from Israel; the other three arrived from different departure points. We found the car and initial guide waiting at the airport. He directed us to our apartment, an upscale, four-bedroom flat with two bathrooms and most facilities, constructed around a large inner courtyard and private swimming pool. The first evening after all arrived, several went out to visit the town and beach. When they returned they were wide-eyed; Ciches was *definitely not* a sleepy fishing town, but rather an international get-away resort whose beaches featured topless women bathers. Nightclubs had an international vacationing, fun-loving population, plus its local residents.

It must be noted that once the beach was discovered, several partners forgot we were here for the sports events, not topless viewing. (Names withheld to protect the parties!) In fact, *I* couldn't get them off the beaches to go to the events in Barcelona. I believe I was the leading sports enthusiast, having always been a sports nut.

We divided the operation into sections.

> Yours truly – food purchasing, housekeeping, and chaffeuring, with the aid of four back-seat drivers.
>
> Larry Roth: Who operates an aluminum smelting operation in Syracuse, NY, appropriately, cooking and food preparation.
>
> Jeff Ram: Photography and eating. Incidentally, he supplied all five participants with a complete photo album at the end.
>
> Jonathan Kaplan: Finance, since he was a senior manager with an MBA at Bank Lyonnaise in New York City.
>
> George Kaplan: The elder statesman and organizer. He would rest.

On arrival, we found the inside balconies had all been festooned with flags: Spanish, Alsatian, French, English. I thereupon decided to display our Israeli banner. On returning from the first day's activity, I found our flag was folded back and not hanging outside. I assumed it was due to wind. The second, third, and fourth days also, our flag was inside each time. Each day I secured it better to avoid the wind on our balcony. One evening while eating dinner, the apartment was suddenly infused with a noxious gas, similar to ammonia. All ran to get out. I, having experienced a number of tear gas operations to disperse criminal mobs in the Old City and at the Kotel, ran to the sink, soaked a towel, covered my face, and began looking for the source of the fumes. They apparently had been sprayed into the Jews' apartment as a warning to keep a lower profile. We reported it to the police next morning and to the house manager, Pedro, who did not accept our story. But you could read in his eyes that he was aware of, and perhaps, a party, to the gas attack.

The Olympic games were something you have to do once in a lifetime. However, on the TV you get a better overall view. Now if you could only eliminate the commercials!

The five of us will never forget the one Shabbos spent together, with only canned food and local vegetables. We located the Habad House in Barcelona (believe it or not) and even found a kosher butcher. So with nothing to lose, we bought a 5-kilogram (11 pound) piece of meat – beef, and Larry Roth made an unforgettable roast beef dinner. I'm sure with Divine Intervention again!

THE HOLIER THAN THOU SYNDROME

Some five years ago, I was traveling to the States on Air France. (My current travel agent, Mordechai Klar, had gotten me a great deal. I'm not a particular fan of France, and over the years, neither have they been of le Juif.)

I was seated in an aisle seat, when the stewardess came around for cocktail orders prior to lunch. I had arranged to be served a kosher meal. I requested a can of tomato juice (some popular brand). Earlier, I had not noticed that across the aisle sat a Haredi gentleman. He now called out to me in a loud whisper.

Haredi: "Reb Yid (fellow-Jew), have you checked the kosher certification on the can?"

YM: "Honestly, no, but I assume on a Tel Aviv-Paris-New York flight it might be beseder. (OK)"

Haredi: "You must be careful. It happens to be my profession. I travel all over the world for the 'OU' (the Union of Orthodox Rabbis, an organization that checks kashrut in food products). I'm returning from the Far East; I just visited several food processing plants over there."

YM: "So why are you going now to the States?"

Haredi: "Our office and my home is in Chicago."

YM: "It's very kind of you to be concerned about my kashrut verification via this tomato juice. But I think perhaps, you are overlooking an even greater mitzvah (commandment) proclaimed directly by our Creator, Lech Lecha. He clearly stated to our Father Abraham in the Torah to 'go up to the land I have given you,' Eretz Yisrael. I've never read anything about checking tomato juice labels. Even the laws on kashrut are not as clearly enunciated as this commandment."

Haredi: "You live in Israel?"

YM: "Yes, in Israel, in Jerusalem, in the Old City. As one of our local rabbis, Shlomo Riskin, has said, 'Aliyah is the mitzvah of our century.' And as the Chofetz Chaim, z"l, exhorted, 'Be certain that what comes out of your mouth is as pure as what goes in it'."

ONLY IN ISRAEL
#12

I had stepped into my Bank Hapoalim branch on Rechov HaPalmach, Jerusalem; as I pulled out of my spot into the traffic flow, an unbelievable sight. A huge white Volvo 940 sedan was headed straight toward me. Two fortunate circumstances came about:

A. The Volvo was moving slowly on this downhill pitched road.

B. My car is light and, having quick reflexes, I swerved to the right, but could not totally avoid contact. The huge Volvo knocked my little Fiat 127 to the side like a toy, and careened downhill. I started to scream at the driver in the offending car. *Shock!* No Volvo driver – the car was rolling unattended. As I now looked into my rearview mirror, it was now crosswise in the road, laterally in free-fall, glancing and hitting several other cars and finally stopping across the way after slamming into another large vehicle, a parked truck. I parked, jumped out of my car (by this time a crowd was at the scene). Suddenly, the offending owner, an older woman driver, approached. On viewing the havoc, she did the smart thing, she fainted. She had left the Volvo double-parked as she ran into a shop to perform an errand. This on an inclined street, unbraked. Attention was now suddenly turned to the driver down on the ground. Someone brought a chair for her to sit on. Another good soul brought out a glass of tea as she was slowly resuscitated and calmed. It was senseless to get involved in the ensuing shouting match. I took the Volvo's license plate number and departed. Yes, her insurance company paid my claim, just another repaired dent in my old beat-up Fiat. At times like that you realize we are really all mishpacha (family).

MY PROGENY –
MY OLDEST DAUGHTER LISA ELLEN

How can one honestly write about one's offspring objectively? The pride in their achievements; the disappointments in their failings. My three are handsome, accomplished and contributing to the societies in which they reside. Personally, I have never lived vicariously through them; perhaps that is how I was able to divorce Lisa and Mitchell's mother, Gloria, and agree to part from Bea and Jackie eight years later.

During 1968-9, I attended a lecture series at the 92nd Street YMHA in Manhattan that featured Dr. Erich Fromm, a noted author and perhaps a guru in his time on human relationships. I came away with a total acceptance of his concept. When children are born, in their first moments as they are exposed to this hostile world we live in, as opposed to the mother's body, they require the most intense and immediate care and attention. From that moment on, the plant (child) must be allowed to flourish by constantly thinning out the relationships; e.g., dense thicket of shrubs inhibits other plants' growth. Also in a parent-child relationship both must be given space to grow. In an orchard, trees are spaced for each to receive their own supply of light and nourishment as required.

Recently I read a commentary that the only connection many American Jews have to their roots are the tunes and a verse in the musical "Fiddler on the Roof." I have to reach the same analogy as Tuvia the Milkman, who witnesses his children disperse from his life and values at a similar level as mine have. And my battle to transcend the generation gap has been lost, leaving permanent wounds and scars.

My First-Born – Lisa Ellen Mink Shulman

Given a name after my mother, Chaya Leah, z"l, Lisa is, objectively, an outstanding individual. She was a superior student from grade school upward. For the past eight years, a medical doctor. Presently an associate professor at her alma mater, the University of Miami Medical School. A neurologist, specializing in Parkinson's Disease. Wife of a physician and successful pediatrician, Peter Shulman, with two sons. Joshua is a pre-med undergraduate at Harvard. Corey's bent seems to be towards the arts. Any father should be proud.

Why are we involved in constant agitation and conflict? In the defense of Lisa:

She has been from birth an outstanding achiever in scholarship, sport, appearance, wife, mother, et al. As such, I believe she would have preferred a father in the professions or on the executive level, leaving daily on the 7:15 a.m. train with a polished leather briefcase, rather than be the junkman's daughter. My divorce from Gloria definitely did not fit into that nice neat package, especially with the ensuing lengthy court battles. Lisa told me long afterwards that she never told her friends about her parents' separation for years and probably didn't admit it to herself, either. During the divorce war years, she became Gloria's champion and made my visitations impossible, in spite of court orders and directives.

Then my marriage to Bea, moving to Israel, assuming an Orthodox religious lifestyle; all acts counter-productive to our relationship. At one point, after spending years chasing the bait of relating to my children, I gave up, when my son, Mitchell was secretly Bar Mitzvahed months prior to the date (while we were in negotiation with my rabbi in Whitestone Queens Jewish Center, Ezra Finkelstein, as intermediary).

For years I had requested the courts to grant me regular visitation privileges. Even with a judge's directives I often came to an empty home. Even when they were home, a hostile Lisa would say, "If you want to take someone out, take the judge." I would go back to the car brokenhearted, at times in tears. But the Bar Mitzvah hurt was unbearable. I decided, for the sake of my sanity and self-respect, I would stop this demeaning, senseless pursuit. Meanwhile, the charges and countercharges in the domestic courts grew many inches higher.

Often I would drive by secretly to catch a glimpse of the children at home or outside walking the dog. That seemed to be the price or penalty imposed on me for leaving the family nest.

In addition, my pain and pining for my children was a constant source of conflict between Bea and myself, as we were now married. One afternoon, after a year and a half's hiatus, while again driving by, I saw Lisa in the kitchen window. I stopped on impulse and she came to the door.

Lisa: "How have you been, Dad?" (Like nothing had happened)

Me: "Would you like to go out for dinner?"

Lisa: "Sure, why not?"

There was a grand reunion. Lisa told me she had been going steady with one Warren Nadel from the area. Mitchell was thrilled to see me again. Warren's father, Leonard, was an executive with the prescribed leather attache case. He worked for Federated Department Stores, was active in synagogue and civic matters, a setting Lisa had always hoped for. I couldn't blame her, and Gloria was super-pleased to be a part of this establishment family group.

At dinner, Lisa suggested I might want to meet Warren N. I arranged a dinner meeting for the following week. We four met at a local restaurant. In a memorable encounter, Warren arrived with a pipe, vest and jacket; I wore a sports shirt. I felt I was being interviewed for the position of future father-in-law. I doubt I fared that well.

After dinner, Warren drove off. Lisa asked if I approved. I was surprised, considering our relatively new relationship. In as charitable a manner as possible I said I felt he was a stuffed shirt and she could do better. Lisa began to rage. "Every worthwhile relationship and part of my life you always destroy. I don't want to see you again!" I was left sitting with Mitchell. He turned to me and said, "I need and love you, Dad. Lisa's only talking for herself."

From that point on my relationship was almost exclusively with Mitchell, as Lisa went off to Buffalo State University, for studies which I subsidized. This was at the height of the anti-establishment, anti-Vietnam War, student rebellion. It didn't bother Lisa at all as she went through four years as a straight A nursing student. Warren attended Carnegie Mellon University for

Engineering in Pittsburgh. I was not invited to Lisa's graduation. It might upset her grandparents who were invited.

Protekzia – Counter-Productive

In the opening paragraph of this chapter, I wrote Lisa is married to Dr. Peter Shulman. That was not a typing error, nor was there a divorce, chas v'sholem (Heaven forbid).

In Israel there is a noun understood at all levels of society – protekzia (ability to get something difficult accomplished by personal clout). Leonard Nadel, Warren's father, was very establishment empowered; he was also on the Board of Trustees of the prestigious Long Island Jewish Hospital. With Lisa's superior grades and inclination to become an I.C.U. (infant care unit) nurse, Leonard was able to get her appointed to that position. But along came that old D.I. again. Dr. Peter Shulman was a new resident in the pediatrics unit. The chemistry of daily contact soon blossomed into a date and eventual romance. So you see, at times protekzia can be counter-productive. And the accusation of my destroying her life was unfair. Perhaps Daddy the Junkman had seen something she overlooked, but first I had to accept another abusive attack and never got praised for my insight. I later heard Warren married a gentile girl, and was not an engineer.

Once Peter Shulman came on the scene and I was able to entertain him and his family, the relationship vis-a-vis Lisa improved. I proposed staging a pretentious kosher wedding celebration in a midtown hotel. Almost two months prior to the wedding's target date, Lisa called. She and Peter would like to visit my home in Hewlett Harbor, Long Island. On arrival, the couple told me and my wife, Bea, that Gloria wanted the wedding at her home. (We were now officially divorced after a five-year struggle, covered in another chapter: Foreclose the House.) There was one *minor point*: my wife, Bea, mother of my two-year old daughter Jackie, *must not attend*.

I asked, "Do you want me to come as a single man, ignoring and insulting the mother of my child? No way!" At this point Lisa became hysterical. I was *again* destroying another part of her life. Crying violently and inconsolable, she

The family at grandson Josh's Bar Mitzvah

suddenly fainted from the pressure. Peter revived her and they both left in a horrible state, amidst renewed shouting and accusations.

A Solomonic Responsum: Make Two Weddings

This was again a major crisis in my renewed relationship with Lisa and I could not attend her wedding.

Again, a point of D.I. In a flash of genius, I came up with the solution to make two weddings. The official one in the afternoon at Gloria's home in Roslyn. Mine, a second wedding the same evening in a midtown hotel. After some difficulty, I contacted Lisa and Peter and presented my idea. After initial shock and extensive rethinking, they agreed, and so it was. The afternoon event was followed by a glorious kosher se'udah at the Plaza Hotel in Manhattan, with two orchestras. The second event was a facsimile of the first, earlier that day. Peter and Lisa exchanged prearranged vows. It was a grand and memorable affair with all the original wedding party, except Gloria, in attendance. I invited 156 relatives and friends for this gala event. The newlyweds had two dinners, two wedding albums, and two exchanges of vows.

The downside was that within a month Bea sued for divorce, despite the efforts I had made to show her respect. The positive side is that the Shulmans are married 24 years after overcoming numerous problems as most couples do. So, two weddings were obviously better than one.

After Peter finished his residence, he joined a burgeoning pediatric practice in southern Florida, Pediatrics Associates. It has since grown significantly, presently with ten offices and thirty physicians. After 20 plus years of practice, Peter is now involved primarily in administration.

About twelve years ago, Lisa decided, after first teaching nursing at a local college, and later attempting to produce a nursing advice spot on a TV show, then teaching the Lamaze birth method, etc., that she wanted the fulfilment of being an M.D. As ever, always striving to reach her maximum. So followed seven years of study – always at the top of the class. Upon graduation (which I *did* attend), rather than becoming a practicing physician in her field of neurology – as stated before, she is presently an associate professor. She travels and lectures, based on the numerous papers she has written on Parkinson's Disease, her area of specialty. That's my daughter, the superstar.

Now to close out the story and bring it up to date.

Trouble at the Bar Mitzvah

By this point, I had married and divorced Hynda, and was married to BatSheva one year.

It was the concurrence of three events: Jackie's High School graduation, Lisa's Medical School graduation, and Joshua (my oldest grandchild's) Bar Mitzvah. All within a month. I must assume responsibility for a portion of the current dispute. I should have recognized the mix of Gloria, Lisa's mother and Joshua's grandmother, and a Bar Mitzvah in a left-wing Reform temple was not a promising setting for an Orthodox Jew. The storm clouds were gathering.

Medical school graduation was memorable. Mitchell had graduated Dental School years before. I was now the proud father of two children with the title "Doctor"; not bad for a second generation junkman. The Bar Mitzvah was a week away. Problem: BatSheva's half-sister had given us her apartment to stay in. The temple was several miles away. Not being able to ride from shul to apartment on Shabbos, we chose to walk back in the hot summer sun. I prearranged to stop off at three lunch spots, and prepaid for drinks.

The Temple Scene

Honestly, I was not surprised at the Saturday morning temple scene: brief praying, the cantor accompanied himself on an electric guitar, the religious leader led the services in English (the T.V. cameras were in operation in the temple). Josh uttered a few Hebrew brachas. At this point an unbelievable occurence! Peter's older brother, Ira, also an M.D., had married again – this time, his former gentile nurse. (Not my problem.) From the bimah, the religious leader called up the people to open the Aron Kodesh (Holy Ark where the Torahs are kept). Who might be designated for this significant ritual? The gentile nurse and her teenage gentile daughter from a previous marriage! At this juncture an uncontrollable force within me called out, "Shiksas opening the Aron Kodesh!" Everyone and everything stopped to look at me. From that point it was all downhill. When the services ended, we went to another hall for the kiddush. I asked the religious leader, "Is anything kosher here?" He responded, "We don't serve kosher food in this temple. It is hypocrisy. Your daughter, Lisa, told me you practice another religious bent." That was my flashpoint. I looked him in the eye and said, "Who the _____ gave you the permission to prostitute our 3,500-year traditions, you lowlife _____?" He promptly turned about and ran to my daughter and said I threatened him physically – *a lie.*

Our relationship never recovered. Three years later, Corey's Bar Mitzvah. I was not invited. Our visits to Florida are, at best, functional, though Lisa did come here three years ago to deliver a paper at a Jerusalem convention on Parkinson's Disease, and we spent some quality time together.

I'm sure we have both suffered from our hostile relationship over the past thirty years. But she's my daughter and I'm very proud of her and admire and love her dearly.

MY SON MITCHELL

My father often referred to me as "My Kaddish"; that meant that after his death I would be the one to say the Kaddish prayer at his graveside and during the following eleven months. At this point, it certainly does *not* seem Mitchell will be my kaddish. Our relationship is now a source of ongoing pain and despair. It certainly didn't begin that way. Mitch was a timid, bright young boy, and when he reached school age, I insisted he attend a Jewish Day School, HANC (Hebrew Academy of Nassau County), where I became an active board member. Years later, Mitch told me of his confusion: learning Torah and Shmirat Shabbat lessons at school, and non-observance of the mitzvahs at home. This was partly my fault. Plus, Gloria was bringing in non-kosher Chinese food, including pork spare ribs, to our home, over my vociferous objections.

For years I know Mitch looked up to me as a figure to emulate, and, I assume, admire. I'm also aware the divorce was especially difficult for him. I can only rationalize; I was living the main years of my life, his were yet to come.

He was ten when I separated from Gloria, a very tender age to stand on his feet and defend his Dad. Afterwards, I learned of his ongoing pain as Gloria, her parents and relatives took target practice on his father for years on end. Gloria immediately withdrew him from the Day School, maybe to get even. Plus, his sister Lisa, a strong-willed individual who gave no quarter in her angry battle to penalize me for dismembering her home. As mentioned previously, the last straw was the secret, pre-date bar mitzvah, where I would be denied even this small naches (pleasure).

It resulted in my discontinuing the visitation rights fight for 1½ years (as covered previously). Once we reopened the door, I saw Mitch regularly, and we became close friends and intimate pals. He spent as much time as possible at my home. We went to professional ball games and events. I was able to play my father role, which I loved. Remember, Lisa was away at Buffalo State University at the time, which meant less interference.

Teenage Years

Mitchell was a well above-average student in a very competitive Roslyn High School class. He was ranked among the top ten students. His older sister Lisa always proclaimed that for raw intelligence (I never knew his I.Q.) Mitch was her superior. (Today she is an associate professor and M.D.)

On graduating from high school, he applied to John Hopkins as a pre-med student and was readily accepted. He also applied for a 6-year combination university B.S. degree and medical school doctoral program at Albany State Medical School. (Incidentally, my sister Selma's son, Cary Lubkin, did accomplish it at Penn State University.)

Mitch was now a full-blown product of the Vietnam War anti-establishment revolt: long hair, scruffy jeans, no interest in appearance. But, in order to help him get into the program, I led him to Barney's Men's Store to buy a preppy blazer outfit. He took a passable haircut and we drove up to Albany, NY, for his interview.

It was a memorable experience for me. The escorting parents and friends were separated from the student applicants and were seated in a small auditorium. One of the administrators addressed us.

"Each one of the students we have invited has the basic brain power to fulfill the demands of this program. What is required is emotional stability and maturity for a six-year total commitment, without summer or winter breaks, to complete this intensive course. It is only by a psychological interview and evaluation that we will attempt to determine which students possess this capability and commitment." Mitchell failed. Eventually the interviewer was proven correct. But Mitch had already been accepted for the Johns Hopkins pre-med program. Following one semester of good grades at Hopkins, he slipped into a phase of partying evenings and weekends, assuming, as he had done in high school, he could cram the night or week before and catch up. It was impossible at a major league university. I went down to Baltimore for a weekend visit when I had heard he was not faring well. Mitch was very distant. However, during the summer breaks he worked for extra money at a factory owned by a friend of mine, at Shea Stadium selling programs, at Madison Square Garden beer sales, and at his friend's father's shoe store, etc. So Mitch was not lazy, just not focused on his future as yet.

At the end of two years, it was apparent that his grades were not at the level for application to a major medical school. He took a leave of absence from Hopkins, and transferred for one year to Buffalo State. He recognized this was at a different level of academia. Mitch returned for his senior year to Hopkins to graduate with his class. In his final year, he again became a straight A student, but, alas, it was too late. One of his partying pals pursued his medical education by applying to Bologna (Italy) Medical school, and spent seven years repeating many classes and is today an M.D.

Mitch now took up a relationship with a New England girl, Amy Strassler. He spent a year in Washington, D.C., working for a health-related Federal Agency. Mitch decided to take the pre-med nationwide exams and scored extremely high. He applied for dental school, and with some protekzia from the Strassler family, he was admitted to the NYU Dental School in NYC. Mitch was now well-focused on becoming a Doctor of Dentistry. He did well scholastically. I met the Strasslers on a visit to the States and their subsequent visit to Israel. I thought his future was set: a Jewish girlfriend and a very affluent establishment family (which can never hurt). But dafka, it didn't happen. After a few years, the couple separated, and my financial support of Mitch became more difficult after my business reverses in Israel. I had set up college funds for both children at their birth, but in Mitch's case, the expenses multiplied as he lived in a mid-town New York apartment. When he was a student, I bought him a new car plus, plus, plus.

But all without regret; after all, this was my son, *my kaddish.*

Hymie (My Father) Junior

Though Mitch was 6'1" and Papa barely 5'2", I found he has many of Papa's traits, but in a larger version. Mitch is quick-tempered; he enjoyed gambling and card playing, had a total disinterest in religious practice, and was a heavy smoker. Yes, truly a Hymie Junior. But as a total package, he is a very handsome, and a kind and sensitive human being.

Clouds on the Horizon

After the break-up with Miss Amy S., Mitch had a number of relationships, several with non-Jewish women. Each time I exhibited my displeasure. After graduation in June, 1982, he began seeking a professional position and found the job market very discouraging. I, from Israel, and on periodic visits, attempted to encourage him. He finally found a professional contact and joined the practice of Dr. Morganstern in White Plains, NY. At the same time, he decided to buy a condominium rather than rent. I paid for the condo and a few years later, when Morganstern offered him an opportunity to buy in, I gave him another major loan (investment).

Mitch was now 34 and I encouraged him to look for a shidduch. He now had a profession, a permanent home, and partnership in an established practice. It was at Lisa's graduation in 1989 that he told me about his special interest in one of his patients. Eventually it surfaced that she was a young non-Jewish woman. I pleaded with him, to no avail. He was in love. I flew to New York to meet the couple. It was senseless to downplay this attractive young doctoral candidate in clinical psychology. We met, and she was both courteous and alert. I posed the question of her converting to Judaism, to which *Mitch* objected. I went a second time prior to their civil marriage, but the die was cast; I could do nothing but tell him I would never accept this union. He is now married seven years, and two years ago they had twins. Though the children are not halachally Jewish, they were named Sara and David. Our relationship is very difficult and has become completely fractured. He maintains contact with his full sister Lisa and half-sister Jackie even more so.

I wish him well, but this rejection of his Jewish heritage is a daily ongoing pain, and for the foreseeable future I've lost my kaddish.

LITTLE JACKIE
(AS I'VE ALWAYS CALLED HER)

Of my three children, Jackie seemed to be tuned in best to my spirit. Possessing her mother Bayla's street smarts and her grandmother (my mother), Chaya Leah's desire to achieve and give.

I've loved and adored Jackie almost from her Day One. Her capability to deal with and relate to the adults in her company on an equal basis, even as a youngster, was always amazing. Jackie was always spirited and positive about life. Her mother chose to sue me for divorce when she was 2½ years old (which I covered in the chapter Bayla, Wife #2). It was difficult for both of us. I was unable to influence her throughout childhood and our father/daughter relationship was strained.

I was able to bring her to Israel for several extended periods of weeks or months, but overall my ability to influence her was limited.

Jackie's scholastic accomplishments were, I feel, an effort to match her half-sister and brother, who were 15 and 20 years older, and her success as a student gave her added confidence in herself. Eventually she gained admittance to the very competitive Stuyvesant High School in Manhattan where she resided. Hence to the University of Wisconsin, and then for a post-grad degree at Tufts University in Boston, MA. In my opinion, her career choice as a school psychologist was greatly influenced by Christine, her brother Mitchell's mate, who has since earned a PhD in psychology. I have continuously stressed to Jackie to be a proud Jew, which seemed at first to bear fruit, when she attended Sunday School in Manhattan after my aliyah. When I lived in the States, after the divorce, I had made it a practice to bring her to Long Island each Sunday morning to attend cheder in my home synagogue. Jackie successfully completed her bat mitzvah ceremony, and we had a lovely party, for which I flew in from Israel.

I was very pleased that her first two serious male relationships were with Jewish young men. Initially at the University of Wisconsin, and subsequently at Boston, while attending post-graduate school, she appeared taken each time with the young men. After Jackie graduated with her master's degree from Tufts, she decided she was better suited to the lifestyle and tempo of Middle America. Let me add that whenever possible, Jackie found part-time work to help defray her schooling and living expenses. After serving an apprenticeship as a school psychologist in a Chicago suburb, called Palatine, for a year, with her knowledge and creative ability she was awarded a position in the Chicago Public School System. Her new job was to deal with problematic teenage students in a program demanding intensive psychological evaluation and therapy. My Jackie had found an avenue to fulfill her wish to give and serve humanity. In addition, she joined, of her own volition, the leading Reform Synagogue in Chicago. I felt secure with her direction and future.

One evening in August 1995, she called from Chicago.

Jackie (while sobbing): "I have been seeing a wonderful young man, but the problem is he is not Jewish, and we just ended our relationship and I'm terribly unhappy."

Dad: "Don't cry. I'll be in Chicago tomorrow. We'll discuss the entire matter."

As promised, the next day I arrived in Chicago. Jackie met me at the airport, and on the way to the apartment (she shared with another single school teacher), she informed me she hadn't really broken the relationship. Jackie explained that after all my years of stressing *only bring me a Jewish young man*, this was the only way she could break the news to me. We spent the next two days together, and she requested I meet Michael. True to her evaluation, he was a fine young man, from a well-structured family, pursuing both accounting and law degrees. The downside was he had completed twelve years of parochial school and was a confirmed, active, observant Catholic, as was his family.

We met at a glatt kosher restaurant in Skokie (a Chicago suburb). I explained my position as an Orthodox observant Jew. I asked whether he would consider conversion. It seems the couple had spent endless hours discussing the various possibilities. The meeting lasted two hours. I was very impressed by Michael, a handsome, respectful and responsible young man. I openly expressed my disappointment that now Jackie might also become a victim of the intermarriage syndrome prevalent in the Western world.

Over the next year and a half, I kept the conversation about her relationship on the back burner, hoping it would go away. In the summer of 1996, when she visited again for two weeks, I stoically avoided the subject. On our return trip to the airport for her departure to the States, Jackie dropped the bomb. "Dad, the relationship is still afloat. We attempted to separate several times unsuccessfully. We love each other. However, Michael is investigating Judaism seriously."

In January 1997, Jackie called to announce her engagement to Michael, which has left me broken-hearted, as of this writing.

THEY WILL NEVER UNDERSTAND US...

So Why Even Try!

After a twenty year aliyah out of Long Island, NY, I've come to the regrettable conclusion that I'll never really be part of the Israeli crowd. I vote, pay taxes, celebrate the national and religious holidays (I consider myself Orthodox), speak my haphazard Hebrew, go to rallies (mostly right-wing), and work hard to fit in. But...

Several Examples

The year is 1976. About 100,000+ *Real Israelis* left our shores for greener pastures after the demoralizing Yom Kippur War: to the USA, South Africa, Canada, Australia, you name it. This Zionist and about 600 others that year made aliyah from the USA. Obviously, going the wrong way. Asked to take a physical exam in Tel Aviv, pre-te'udat oleh. I'm ushered into a *psychologist's* office. He inquires, "Why did you choose to come to Israel now??!!"

Business

I was brought up in the scrap business. I have thirty years' personal business experience and can validate this, having built (with partners) a very successful scrap operation on Long Island (Cousins Metal). My misfortune was being introduced to a scrap dealer of sorts, at a business gathering in NY. I was invited to see his operation in Tel Aviv and Ashdod. I was amazed. They were about

50-100 years behind the times; burlap bags for shipping; wicker baskets for sorting, metal wheelbarrows; and 90% donkey work (schlepping)!

A big challenge: I'm going to show them how it's done today!

Two years later and a tale which should bring tears to the eyes of any compassionate soul. My tale of woe fighting KOOR (Kiryat Pladot of Steel City), Ministry of Industry, dishonest and dishonorable associates, the Real Israelis and 40-50% inflation at the time; I was separated from about 40% of my net worth. The story in detail was told to both Martha Meisel and David Krivine, both fine journalists with the Jerusalem Post, now departed, who recorded it for posterity.

Sanitary Habits

Discarding garbage on the streets. Smoking in public offices, banks, post offices, etc. When you bring it to the attention of the Real Israelis you are probably told to go back to America. (They hear my accent.)

If you challenge a political figure (even our former Prime Minister Peres) you can also hear, go back where you came from, as Ruth Matar, an activist from NY, and founder of Ladies in Green, will validate. Of course, Peres is originally from Poland, like my forebears.

So what the hell am I doing here after twenty years?

Somehow, I feel I belong here just as much as the *Real Israeli*. I love this country and what we've accomplished after 49 years of independence. I look at the military who really sacrifice years and unfortunately lives and feel a kinship to them.

BUT MOSTLY, IT'S EASIER TO ACCEPT, *"GO BACK TO AMERICA,"* THAN SOME REDNECK CALLING YOU *"DIRTY JEW."*

ONLY IN ISRAEL
(AND JERUSALEM)

The date Friday, April 18, 1997, was the time of a major political crisis.

Background: the Bar-On affair had been vibrating for three months. The police, in an act contrary to established procedure, had leaked their recommendation to indict the five major players in the saga as conspirators:

Prime Minister Benjamin Netanyahu

Recently appointed and youthful Justice Minister Hanegbi

The Director-General of the Prime Minister's office Avigdor Liebermann

A blustering supposed political kingmaker and businessman, David Appel

The manipulative and mysterious leader of the ten-man Knesset Shas party faction, "Mr. Teflon" Aryeh Deri.

Three months earlier the TV news had fired a political bombshell. It claimed that Deri and the attorney-general appointee, a nondescript Jerusalem attorney and Likud party activist, Ronni Bar-On (called in America a political hack) had prior to his appointment cut a deal. Deri's fraud case, which was pending and wandering through the courts for three and a half years, would be dismissed, based on a technicality, when Bar-On took office as attorney-general, despite the mountains of testimony, affidavits and evidence. The Cabinet approved the appointment and the next day, based on this TV expose, Bar-On resigned under a significant foul-smelling aroma.

The newly-appointed, religiously observant and highly respected attorney-general, Elyakim Rubinstein, and the State prosecuting attorney, Edna Arbel were now pressured to make a decision whether or not to indict. They decided to present their decision on Sunday, the twentieth of April. Returning to the established axiom that Jews are News, every news service, major newspaper, TV and cable service world-wide were waiting for their decision. This in a nation of four and a half million Jews in a country the size of the United States state of New Jersey. Ludicrous isn't it?

Back to our story.

That Friday evening, BatSheva and I had been invited to the home of Jeff and Diane Ram. On our arrival, Jeff informed me that erev Shabbos he prayed at a small local shtibel (small synagogue) in the heart of Jerusalem. On entering this modest, converted three room apartment in a local residence, I looked around the minyan for a familiar face. Up front was my friend Yehuda Weinstock – successful real estate agent and seriously wounded hero of the Yom Kippur War. To my left sat the manager of my Bank Leumi branch. To my right and a row back was the renowned physicist from M.I.T. (Massachusetts Institute of Technology) Professor Jerry Schroeder, now a local resident and lecturer. Totally unobtrusively on a back bench sat Attorney-General of the State of Israel Elyakim Rubinstein, intensively absorbed by his Shabbos prayers. All were part of an unpretentious local minyan. Observant Jews for whom the week's activities were in recess. It was now Shabbos.

REVIEWING ONE'S LIFE

One of my rabbis, attempting to explain the ultimate disaster in our lifetime – the Shoah[1] – drew an analogy. Hashem has an advantage over man: He can look down from the heavens and, in one sweep, view the entire history of the world from creation to the end of times. Men can view and absorb small bites of history and draw conclusions based on current events of, at most, 3,000-4,000 years.

It is also of interest, as a person draws in the home stretch of his lifespan in this world, that it is possible to review the entire picture in fast forward. How did I ever make a stupid decision like that? How fortunate I was to survive that situation, including three major auto collisions – to walk away uninjured. If only I had said or done this, bought that, sold what have you, etc. For a person married 5 times, plus many relationships, these queries are a challenge to one's ego.

The only solution is to thank Hashem for your years and ask forgiveness for your failings.

---

1. Shoah – the Holocaust.

EPILOGUE

The details of my life's story have been mostly recorded and edited for posterity. However the balance of sand in my hourglass continues to run out at a slower pace and with a significantly diminished reserve.

My older daughter, Lisa Shulman, now associate professor at the University of Miami Medical School, continues to forcefully pursue her profession. My son, Mitchell, now a successful dental practitioner in White Plains, NY, has had twins, Sara and David, who are not halachically Jewish.

My major disappointment, my dearly beloved daughter, Jackie, now a successful school psychologist in the Chicago public school system, announced her engagement to the Christian Michael Gleason in January, 1997.

My grandchildren, Corey and Joshua Shulman are in full pursuit of successful careers. Corey, the younger son, is an art student at the prestigious Rhode Island School of Art and Design. Joshua has been accepted to Harvard Medical School after four outstanding undergraduate years. He was also invited to spend a year in Cambridge University in England as a visiting scholar.

NOT BAD, ZADAH NAHUM HAIM, ONLY FIVE GENERATIONS FROM A SHTIBEL IN POGROM-RIDDEN BIALYSTOK TO A CAMBRIDGE SCHOLAR!

For the past ten years I have been plagued by a business associate here in Israel, Eliezar Kabbasi. It has resulted in endless lawsuits and counter-suits.

The gemach fund continues to prosper with available funds now at a quarter of a million dollars. This necessitates ten to fifteen hours a week of labor.

My marriage to BatSheva is moving under its own steam. To quote her, she is in second place on longevity in the marriage race. First position is still held by Gloria, now retired in Florida, at fifteen years. With nine years to BatSheva's credit, with the help of Hashem, she will reach the point of attaining first place.

It will be really sad to leave this world. There is so much more to do, learn and experience.

SOME BRIEF THOUGHTS AND COMMENTS

A clever decal on a car: Will Rogers Never Met a Lawyer.

Rifka, a neighbor, says that her children have laid so many trips on her she decided to open a travel agency.

Rabbi Nachman Kahane: "The Jews were once considered bookworms; now they are tapeworms."

Rabbi Nota Schiller, Ohr Sameach: "The reasons the digital watch is so popular today: One sees just *this moment* in time, not where we come from or where we are going, as on the fully numbered watch face."

The only sure formula for profit in the stock market is to follow my actions carefully:

    Whatever I sell, buy at once.

    Whatever I buy, sell at once.

Harry Truman, the 33rd president of the USA, made these two memorable statements.

1. The buck stops here.
2. I'll only accept one-armed members into my cabinet. Hence they can never say, "On the other hand."

Seventy Years of Observations:

The eyes are the windows of the soul.

The tongue is the pen of the heart.

On Getting Old:

Everything aches at first occasionally, then constantly.

You know you're getting older when every time you enter a room you are the Senior Citizen.

On impulse, most people will respond that the opposite of pain is joy.
Ask someone in pain; He'll answer, just relief from pain.

A basic difference between Israeli and American society:

In the States, it's taboo to discuss religion and politics in general conversation. In Israel, it's the only things you talk about.

Friends are similar to a savings account. You deposit good deeds and kindness and hope that when you need to make a withdrawal, there will be an available balance.

An acquaintance told me his daughter graduated university as an economist. He contacted several business friends to assist her in finding a position in her field. Finally, one agreed. "Yes, I can use an economist who can type, file, take dictation and make coffee on demand."

Others:

Aliyah is the mitzvah of our century.

To waste a mind is a crime.

I'm too big to cry, but old enough to know that it hurts.

If mitzvahs were that easy, everyone would do them.

We all perform many demonstrative acts for our public, assuming our every action is being carefully observed, when suddenly the theater lights are turned on and we realize there is really no one out there.

The Big Apple excitement is all about getting turned on. When you're involved in the Torah world, you're tuned in constantly. Therefore, no highs and lows.

Be certain that what comes out of your mouth is as pure as what goes in it.

Photographs

THE YECHEZKEl

Joshua
Corey

Lisa
& Peter
Shulman

Mitchell

Jaqueline
Leah

Gloria
Stamberg

Beatrice
Siflinger

K

Larry, **❍**
& Ad**a**

Selma (**s**
& Art**…**
LUBK**…**

Shelly
& Sue

Norman
& Sandy

Suzy
& Arnold
STEIGER

Nicole
& Jack
KERMAN

Suzette
& Max

Faigel

Rivkah

George
& Edith
GERING

Jeanette
& Michah
EPSTEIN

Renie
& Jacque

Dorothy
& George
MANN

Lillia**n**

Nachum Chaim
& Shoshana
GERING
(BIALYSTOCK)

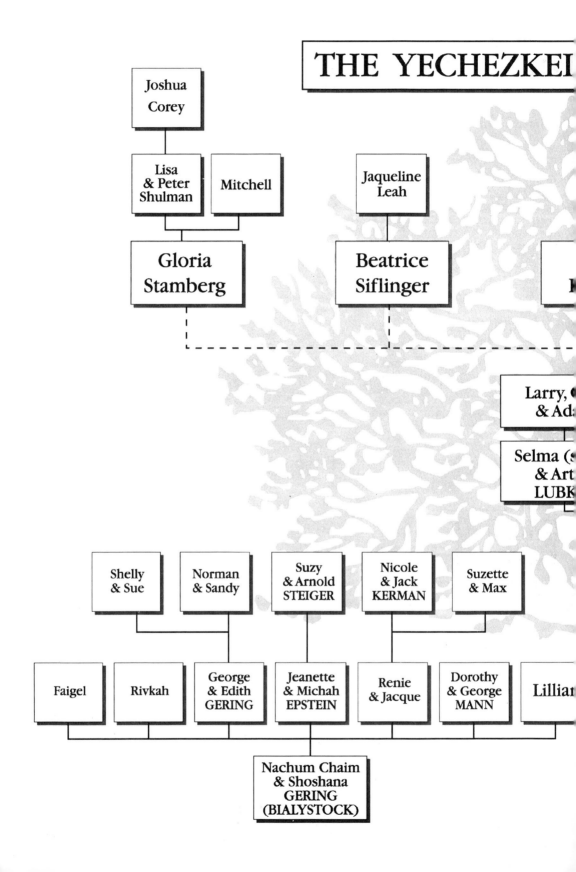